THE STORY OF WINDS

Maurice Bond CB, MVO, OBE.

The Story of WINDSOR

LOCAL HERITAGE BOOKS
Newbury, Berkshire

Acknowledgements

The publishers are greatly indebted to Gordon Cullingham and Raymond South for their invaluable help during the preparation of this book for publication, following the death of Maurice Bond.

The cover illustration is of Peascod Street at the turn of the century.

FIRST PUBLISHED 1984

LOCAL HERITAGE BOOKS
3 Catherine Road, Newbury, Berkshire
and 36 Queens Road, Newbury, Berkshire

ISBN 0 86368 010 0

Produced through MRM (Print Consultants) Ltd., Reading, Berkshire.
Printed in England by Unwin Brothers Ltd., Old Woking, Surrey.

Contents

References		8
The origins of Windsor		10
The Castle in the Middle Ages		19
The Mediaeval Town		33
Tudor and Stuart Windsor		51
Georgian Windsor		68
The Victorian Castle		81
Victorian Windsor		89
i	Urban development	89
ii	Local government	96
iii	The Railways	98
iv	The Churches	104
v	The Arts	115
vi	The Schools	120
vii	Sport	127
viii	Members of Parliament	131
The Castle in the 20th century		134
The Borough in the 20th century		142
i	At the turn of the century	142
ii	The Edwardian Age	145
iii	The First World War	150
iv	Between the Wars	153
v	The Second World War	157
vi	Re-organisation	161

Part of Collier's plan of Windsor made in 1742.

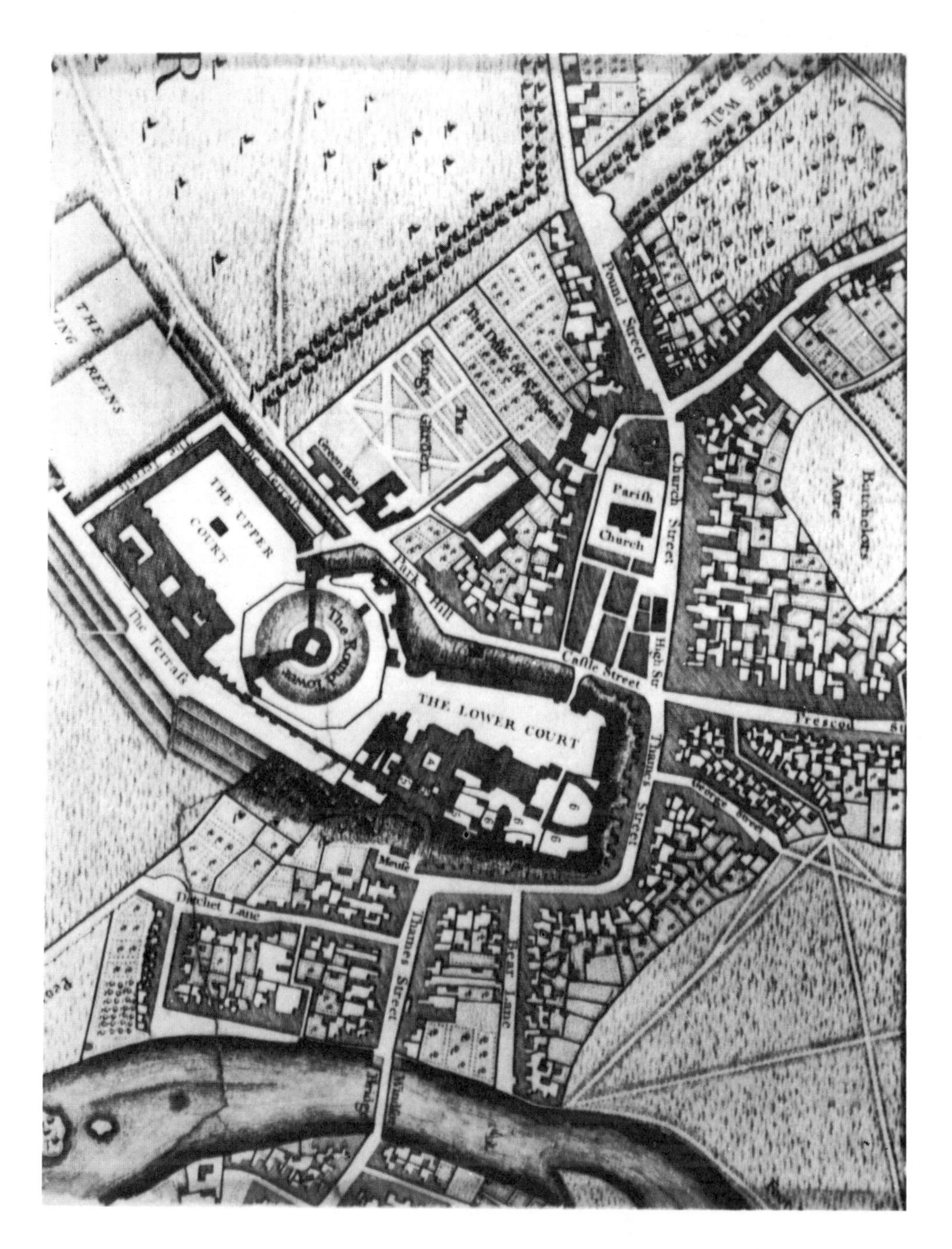

THE UPPER COURT
The Round Tower
THE LOWER COURT
The Terrass
Parish Church
Church Street
Pound Street
Castle Street
High Str
Thames Street
Park Hill
Batchelors Acre
Datchet Lane
Bear Lane
Mews
Green Hou.
The Kings Garden
George Street

References

At the end of each chapter references are provided to the main manuscript of printed sources on which the chapter is based. The suprascript numerals in the text guide the reader to the appropriate reference.

For these the following abbreviations are used:

BAJ	*Berkshire Archaeological Journal* (originally the *Berks, Bucks and Oxon Archaeological Journal*), (1895 –)
BRO	The Berkshire Record Office, Shire Hall, Reading.
RF St G	*The Annual Reports of the Society of the Friends of St George and the Descendants of the Knights of the Garter* (1932 –).
Handlist	M. and S. Bond, *Handlist of Records preserved in the Muniment Rooms of the Royal Borough of New Windsor* (1973).
Harwood	T.E. Harwood, *Windsor Old and New* (1929); the notes on which this work was based are in the British Library, Add MSS 41764, 41765.
Hope	W.H. St John Hope, *Windsor Castle, An Architectural History*, 2 volumes and plates.
M St GC	*Monographs concerning St George's Chapel, Windsor Castle* (1939 –).
TD	R.R. Tighe and J.E. Davis, *Annals of Windsor*, 2 volumes (1858).
VCH	*The Victoria County History of Berkshire*, volume i (1906), ii (1907), iii (1923).
WEE	*The Windsor Slough and Eton Express* (1812 –).

The Origins of Windsor

Windsor is famous as the seat of the largest and most continuously occupied castle in the world. Its dramatic outline, culminating in the Round Tower, can be seen from miles around and is one of the first identifying features for many air-travellers as they approach London's airport. To Osbert Sitwell as a boy Windsor seemed 'a legendary gothic city upon its hill' and, as he contemplated its significance, 'the chief repository of English history and tradition', where local colour of every age lingers and still has a meaning.'[1]

Yet its very earliest days were unpromising. For thousands of years – in fact from the Neolithic period to the time of the Roman invasion – the whole of this part of the Thames valley was somewhat uninviting. thick damp oak forests, interspersed with barren heaths, came down to a wide river area with erratic flooding capacity.[2] Early man travelled across the Windsor area, leaving behind him numerous artifacts, from stone axe-heads to bronze swords and spear-heads, but there is little evidence of settlement, apart from what seems like a Bronze Age site at Runnymede now being investigated. Also, a Bronze Age, if not Neolithic, interrupted ditch enclosure found recently at Eton Wick may be comparable to the Windmill Hill seasonal meeting places. Historians have, however, been over-ready to assume that 'civilised' life in England began in Roman or perhaps in Saxon times, and Peter Fowler has recently reminded us that the clearing of the natural wilderness began as early as 5000 BC, and that much of England was under cultivation in fields by 1500 BC.[3]

There may therefore still be much to discover about the origins of the settlements in the Windsor area. But at the moment the historian's starting point is clear. It is physically just outside the present town, on the edge of the village to the south-east still known as Old Windsor. The visitor, after crossing the Long Walk, with its spectacular view of the Castle on his left, travels along a straight road, 'Albert Road' (constructed in Prince Albert's time) which divides the royal farm and gardens from open arable land on the right. Half a mile along, in the middle of the arable, is a wooded clump which protects a quadrangular moated site, Tile Place Farm. Here, in 1865, were found two Roman tile tombs, illustrated here, one containing burnt bones and finely decorated pottery.[4] More recent finds in the vicinity, of Roman tiles, pottery and building material, make it likely that in this area there was an important early settlement. Not, of course, in Tile Place Farm, for burials were not made in the centre of a Roman villa or town, but more probably nearer the river, another half-mile on. Very likely the settlement was an isolated farm. This would have involved the erection of timber or

Roman tile tombs found in 1865 at Tile Place Farm.

stone buildings with tiled roofs, the growth of wheat crops, and the keeping of horses, cattle, sheep and (always a local speciality) pigs. It is possible that this Roman farm had had a slightly earlier origin. The Romans might have taken over a Celtic farmstead, in the same way that the Celtic capital at Silchester had been by 75 AD. made into a Roman fort, 'Calleva of the Atrebates'. In any case, the farm hands of Windsor would have been Celts, and, more specifically, Celts of the tribe of the Atrebates. The Windsor area was at the furthest easternmost point of the region occupied by this tribe – a frontier area or, at any rate, a disputed area, as it was to remain for some centuries.

When the Roman rulers left Britain in 410 AD. this Windsor homestead might have continued until the Saxon invaders finally settled in the area. We do not know. There is a continuing discussion about the effect of the Roman withdrawal from Britain. Did society more or less collapse, or did Romano-Britons continue to farm and trade, as the towns slowly fell into decay?

Our next evidence at Windsor only came to light fairly recently. To see it in its context it is necessary to go a little further away from Windsor and Tile Place Farm, to the end of Albert Road (with its last glimpse of the Castle), turn right and then, in 200 yards, left along a road signposted 'To the Church'. Half a mile down this road, on the bank of the Thames, is a field still known as 'Kingsbury' (that is, the King's Town), part of the general area which was described as 'Windsores' in the Domesday Book of 1087. Excavations carried out by Dr Brian Hope-Taylor between 1953 and 1958, followed by geophysical and resistivity surveys, make it certain that here is a major Anglo-Saxon site, one of the most important in the country. Any full description must await Dr Hope-Taylor's publication of his report on this major archaeological undertaking, which is now nearing completion. His interim accounts, however, give a clear general picture of Windsor's early development. Dr Astill's diagram delineates the area with which he is dealing.

Three phases in its development are proposed. An original settlement on the banks of the Thames may perhaps be dated to years round 600 AD. Further expansion took place between 650 and 750; and then an outstanding change came in phase III, say 750 – 850. During this time a large and sophisticated mill was constructed, with three vertical water-wheels working in parallel and served by a great channel of the river, dug by the Saxons across the neck of a loop in the Thames within which the site lies. The channel was ¾ mile long, over 20 feet wide, and up to 12 feet in depth – for those days, a mighty work. The timbers of the mill itself were identified, and close to it was a stone building which seems to have had glazed windows (again, unusual) and a tiled roof. We know that by the 1040s the Kings of England had this 'Windsores' as a royal residence. 'Phase III' may perhaps mark the adoption of Windsores for such a purpose.

Around 900 AD there is evidence of widespread destruction by fire, perhaps as the result of a Viking raid, but life continued on quite a grand scale, with a remaking of the water-channel and the construction of a timber building on sleeper beams, say in the late 900s. One of the most interesting finds was of a gilt-bronze sword-guard, which can be dated just before the Norman Conquest. Others include cooking pots of the 800s, bone pottery burnishers and bone weaving-picks, combs made of bone but riveted with iron, bronze cloak pins, a Saxon saucepan or pipkin, of about 800 AD, and prick spurs from the 11th and 12th centuries, one with inlaid silver ornament beneath a corroded surface.

How does this impressive opening to Windsor's history relate to that of the nation? We shall probably never know precisely who the first Saxon settlers at Windsor were, but Margaret Gelling is quite clear that Berkshire at a relatively early stage had been conquered by the Middle Saxons, that is, the Kingdom of Mercia, probably during the 700s AD. The southern boundary of Berkshire (which comes practically to the southern edge of Saxon Windsor where it joins the Thames) may be an arbitrary boundary laid out by the Mercian Kings when they retained part of their province south of the Thames after the defeat at Ellundun in 825 by the Kingdom of Wessex.[7] So Windsor could have started as a Mercian settlement; but Egbert of Wessex (802 – 839) became, in effect, the overlord of all the English people, as well as the chief opponent of the Danes (who had begun their forays into England in 790 and continued for a century). In 871 Alfred the Great became king and, after fierce fighting, established some sort of peace with the Danes by 878. It is not unreasonable to consider the strengthening of Windsor after 750 as part of a Mercian effort to hold on to a distant part of their territory against the formidable power of Wessex. It would have passed eventually into the hands of Egbert (the period of phase III) and, above all of Alfred the Great.

Windsor was some sort of tribal or national defensive position for the Saxons, justifiably described as a burh or fortified town. It continued through the reigns of Ethelred the Unready (978 – 1016) and Canute (1016 – 1035), then emerging into documentary history when a chronicler described King Edward the Confessor (1042 – 1066) as healing the blind in the royal palace of Windsor, and a new abbot of St Augustine's Abbey was being consecrated at Windsor on St Augustine's day, 1061.[8]

The unified Saxon kingdom of England was overthrown at the Battle of Hastings in 1066, but initially a new Norman regime made little difference to Windsor. William the Conqueror continued his predecessors' tradition, using Kingsbury, its church and surrounding buildings as a council place and a hunting centre. He became, in fact, so attracted to it that he reversed a grant by Edward the Confessor of January 1066 by which the Confessor had given the ownership of Windsor to his beloved new Benedictine Abbey of Westminster. The Conqueror set it out in terms in a charter: 'By the constitution and favour of the venerable Abbot of Westminster, I have agreed for Windlesora for the king's use, the place appearing proper and convenient for a royal retirement on account of the river and its nearness to the forest for hunting, and many other royal conveniences, in exchange for which I have given Wokendune and Feringes'. So, by the end of 1066 Windsor began a continuous and documented royal connection which has lasted to this day.

This Windlesora was the area of the Saxon settlement, centering on the riverside area of the present village of Old Windsor 1½ miles away, and certainly not part of the royal exchange with Westminster. It was what would have looked like downland, an open grass hill, an outlier of the chalk North Downs. This hill rises 100 feet sheer above the Thames and on two other sides has a sharp ascent. There was probably a hamlet, known as Orton, on its east slopes, but the main part of the hill lay in the parish of Clewer. Within about four years of his accession William had decided that this dominant cliff would provide the western-most of a circle of defensive posts, the new-fangled 'castles' (unknown to Saxons) with which he was

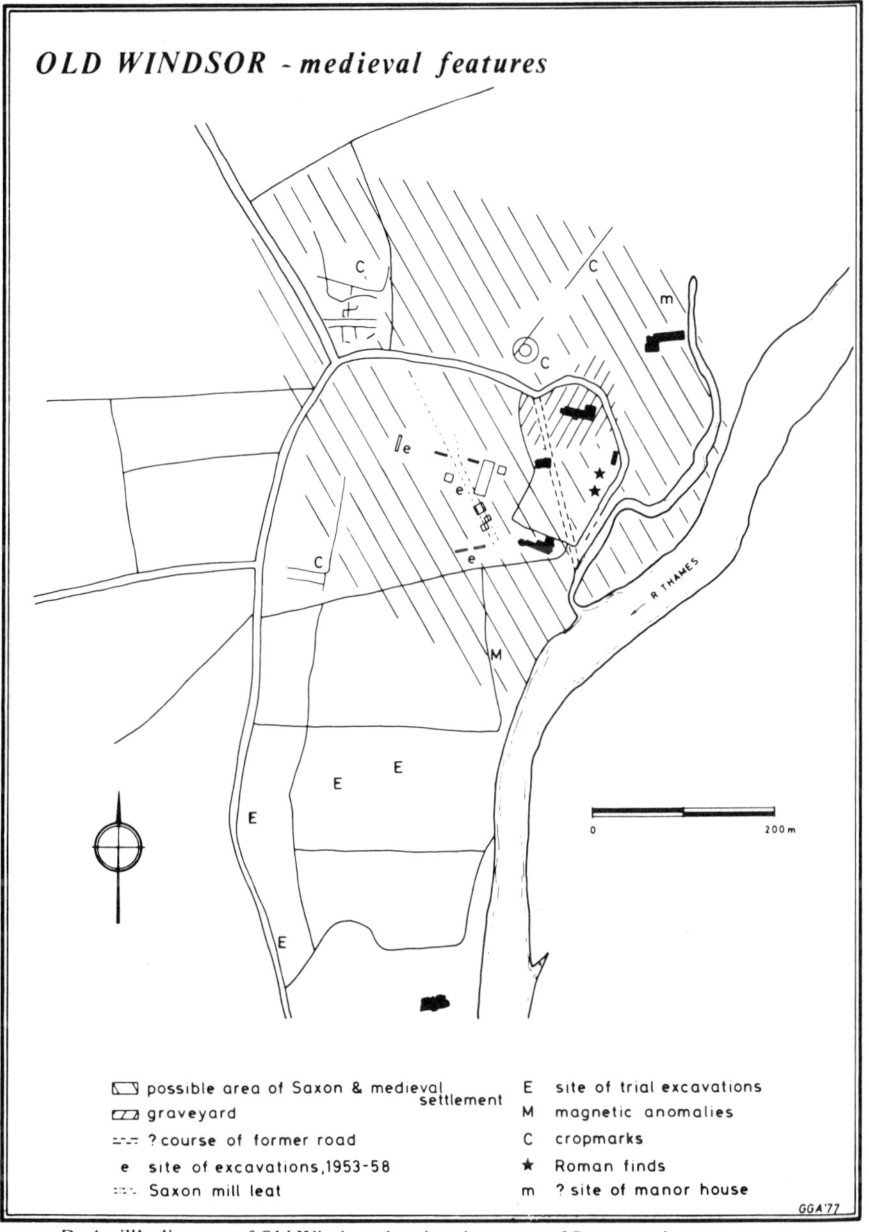

Dr Astill's diagram of Old Windsor showing the extent of Saxon settlement.

encircling his capital city of London, his 'great scheme for rendering permanent the Conquest of England'. From a strategic point of view the Clewer downland was ideal. It was 'the one strong point between London and Wallingford where a fortress could be placed to guard the waterway of the Thames', and it was equidistant from London with William's other castles: Ongar, Hertford, and Pleshey on the north; Rayleigh and Rochester on the east; Tonbridge and Reigate on the south, with Berkhamstead at the north-west point and Guildford at the south-west. And all roughly within a day's easy march from the capital. Windsor closed the ring of castles round London.

The date of the fortification at Windsor is not precise, but it may well have been in about 1070. Then the Conqueror had ditches dug round Clewer hill, palisades erected on the edges, and a central inner defensive mound established. Rather as William had had to regain 'Old' Windsor from Westminster Abbey, so in order to construct Windsor Castle he had to regain the hill at Clewer, for at the Conquest he had granted the lordship of Clewer to a Norman follower, Ralf, son of Seifride. Clewer parish continued for centuries to extend to the foot of the Castle hill, and the north-west tower built in 1240 (now the Curfew Tower) was at first known as the Clewer tower. The royal estates now had two centres: Clewer hill and the long-established *burh* 1½ miles downstream. Together they were still simply known as 'Windsor'; for the Normans there was no 'New' or 'Old' Windsor.

The name deserves attention. Mediaeval chroniclers, even Popes, misunderstood it, thinking 'Windsor' indicated the 'sore wind' (*ventus morbidus*) blowing across the castle hilltop. Etymologists then suggested that the normal latin spelling of *Windlesora* meant a river bank (*ora*) with a meandering or winding course. Nowadays it seems fairly certain that the name means a bank with a windlass (in Anglo-Saxon, *windels*).[9] This is significant for the whole of Windsor's development. It would suggest that here rather than above or below on the Thames was a point of transshipment at which goods were brought ashore. This would not be for dispersal in the interior, since six miles lower down, at Staines, boats would have passed the main Roman road to the west. But there would have been a major demand at Windsor for imported goods; and if Windsor was an important royal residence this would have been particularly so. It is notable that among pottery found at (Old) Windsor is a pitcher identified as having come from the Rhineland – in addition to other sherds conforming to contemporary East Anglian styles.[10]

A final point of interest about the name is that, as in the case of the neighbouring township of Clewer (Clivore), it is a hybrid of Anglo-Saxon and Latin. This suggests in each case some continuity from Romano-British times to the seventh century barbarian settlement.[11]

An aerial view of Windsor Castle and the Long Walk. The Walk is three miles long, and was planted with elms in 1685. These trees were felled in 1945.

References

1 O. Sitwell *The Scarlet Tree* (1946), 257
2 *The Middle Thames in Antiquity* ed. R.F. Denington and S. Morgan (1966), 17: 'Many more examples (of pottery finds) are known from the north bank of the Thames than from the south bank, from which it can be deduced that the dry heaths of the gravel terraces were preferable to the wet clay land of oak forest'.
3 See the general survey by Clive H. Knowles, *Landscape History* (1983) 21.
4 VCH, i, 219.
5 This resulted from the then Vicar of Old Windsor, the Reverend A.L. Coombs, alerting

myself in September 1951 to the discovery of Roman pottery in sewage trenches being dug within his parish. Thanks to prompt action by the Honorary Secretary of the Berkshire Archaeological Society, Maitland Underhill, detailed investigations were arranged which resulted in 1953 in the beginning of Brian Hope-Taylor's extensive and productive excavations.

6 See 'Excavations at Kingsbury, Old Windsor', BAJ (1954 – 5). 147, and the fuller report in *Medieval Archaeology* (MA), ii (1958), 183 – 5; also a letter from BHT to Maitland Underhill, 20 March 1956.

7 M. Gelling *Place Names of Berkshire*, iii (1976), 841 – 4.

8 For the detailed history of Windsor under the Confessor and the Conqueror, see Hope, 114, and Hanwood, 60 – 63.

9 Gelling, op.cit., i (1973), 27.

10 MA, 184.

11 The early development of Windsor has recently been summarised by Mrs Judith Hunter in *The Changing Face of Windsor* No 1 *The Beginnings* (1977), a publication of the Windsor Local History Publications Group.

The Castle in the Middle Ages

The Castle at first was obviously dependent on the royal manor to the south east, but by the 1200s two Windsors, Old and New, had come into existence. William's motte-and-bailey defensive fort, within a generation or so, became a major royal residence. Some of his timber and wattle structures were replaced by stone,[1] and the Anglo-Saxon Chronicle records that at Whitsuntide in 1110 Henry I 'held his court for the first time in the new Windsor'. Still more strikingly, the King's marriage took place in a Castle chapel in 1121; the Queen was consecrated and crowned there, and archaeological evidence at the Saxon royal residence indicates that much of the occupation at 'Old' Windsor by the court ceased soon after. In the Pipe Roll of 1130 – 31 New Windsor is explicitly described as *burgus*, a borough; and some of the old Saxon *burh* became an empty field, still called 'Kingsbury', the name it retains to this day.

There were four stages in the development of the Castle after the Norman period. First, in the 12th century Henry II built a Great Hall in the Lower Ward (where 'Denton's Commons' now are) and he reconstructed the Castle's exterior and internal wooden defences in stone, adding the characteristic rectangular towers: this, between 1173 and 1179. Secondly, in the thirteenth century, his grandson, Henry III, a passionate builder who inherited a castle that had been twice besieged, erected a massive curtain wall with three drum towers (1230) on the west beyond the Norman wall which he demolished. He thus extended the Conqueror's ground-plan westwards. In addition, Henry III built two lavish and separate royal lodgings, one in the Upper Ward (where the State Apartments now are), the other in the Lower Ward (subsequently replaced by the Canons' Cloisters). He also built the large chapel dedicated to St Edward the Confessor in the Lower Ward which was to become the first St George's Chapel in 1348 (finally in the nineteenth century reconstructed as the Albert Memorial Chapel).

Thirdly, Henry's great-grandson, Edward III, in the fourteenth century remade the royal lodgings in the Upper Ward and established a college of secular canons in the Lower Ward, with two cloisters, a treasury and two chapter houses, one for the canons, the other for the Order of the Garter whose services and festivals were usually held within the college area. Finally, in the fifteenth century, when Edward IV considered he had triumphed over his Lancastrian rivals and had established a new royal dynasty that would rule England for generations, he sought to make the Castle the dynastic centre and burial place for himself and his descendants. The old chapel of 1240 was abandoned and in its place a grand new structure rose, the most daring and lavish piece of royal building of his day, the present St George's Chapel (1475), although neither he nor his dynasty was to survive to see the final stones inserted, half a century later, under the Tudor King Henry VIII in 1528.

By these four stages of development the Castle became remarkable – '*quo non erat ad id tempus splendidius infra fines Europae*' ('than which there was no more splendid within the bounds of Europe').

The Castle had become a great royal residence, but its primary purpose was as a fort and its commanding officers the Constables were, as Shelagh Bond has shown, military leaders of eminence as well as administrators of a wide forest area.[2] The Castle served as a look-out post and as a garrison from which soldiers could emerge when needed. The Norman royal castles were in fact so overwhelming in their new and unexpected impact that like the proverbial policeman on the beat their mere existence tended to preserve law and order. It seems likely that in the whole of the Middle Ages there were only three 'high cost' sieges of English castles,[3] yet Windsor had its share of less costly but nationally significant sieges. In 1193 Richard Coeur de Lion was on crusade. His brother John attempted to seize the crown. The Justiciar of the realm, the Archbishop of Rouen, conserving his resources, decided to let John take Windsor. Other magnates resented this and decided to oust John from Windsor. A chronicle simply records that they besieged the Castle with an innumerable multitude of knights and foot soldiers. The siege lasted nearly two months and Windsor was 'almost captured' when John's men in the Castle gave up and surrendered.[4]

Within a generation, ironically enough, the exact opposite occurred. John had succeeded to the throne, to find ever-increasing forces arrayed against him. In 1215 he went from Windsor Castle to Runnymede to agree to the capitulation we know as Magna Carta. This, however, did not bring peace. In May 1216 French forces landed to help the barons resist John. On 24th June they besieged Dover Castle, and about four days later a baronial army besieged Windsor Castle, which was defended, not by John (who was at Corfe) but by Engelard de Cygony, constable of the Castle 'a man very skilful in the art of war', with 60 knights and many more footsoldiers. For nearly three months the Castle was attacked. Engelard's men repeatedly made sorties in order to drive the attackers from the walls. By September one chronicler says the Castle was on the point of surrender; another claims that John bribed the attackers 'who withdrew by night from the siege, leaving their tents behind' in order to chase John's own army into East Anglia – where on the night of 18 – 19 October John died, after, it seems, a surfeit of peaches and beer. Unlike the first Windsor siege, that of 1216 appeared to have failed, but the fact of three months' delay had certainly weakened John's strategy.[5]

What did these two sieges mean for Windsor? Firstly, destruction within

the Castle. After 1193 gates, bridges, and residences had to be repaired and only in 1196 was the castle in good order again. The damage of 1216 was still greater. The walls were partly destroyed and it was not until 1230 that the new western wall was completed with the three drum towers, all of which still stand above the town of Windsor.

This we know from the royal accounts. What can only be surmised is the effect on the town. The traders who came to New from Old Windsor had settled on the west and south side of the Castle – precisely where the besieging armies would encamp, and across which the siege engines would be dragged to be set up against the castle walls. Fields and orchards would be raided for food; stones and arrows would descend from the castle. Fires would start from the sulphur, quicklime, pitch, and red-hot sand which were essential parts of siege attack and defence. The town, inevitably built of highly inflammable materials, must by 1217 have been almost derelict. However, as we shall see, the developing life of the castle under its new king, Henry III (1216 – 1272) clearly brought a rapid revival. Windsor was not destroyed; and in fact his reign marked the general establishment of a town-plan which was to continue, little altered, until the early 1800s. Probably the people of Windsor themselves, with their pigs and sheep, had survived by crowding into the castle, possibly helping to man the walls. They would certainly have been safer inside than outside the walls.

Some military incidents occurred later in Windsor's history, but as a medieval fort Windsor Castle by 1216 had passed its prime. Its continuous life thereafter was as a home for the royal family, as an urban settlement in itself, something of a separate walled town living its own vigorous and independent life. It has never joined that large group of castles of which James Pope-Hennessy not unfairly commented 'we are haunted by a perpetual doubt . . . How are we to believe that these places were ever other than we see them today, chilly and lifeless?'. Windsor is not in the class of Avignon or Les Baux.

The new era of the royal home was happily inaugurated when in 1239 the young Queen, Eleanor of Provence, gave birth in the Castle to her first-born son, the future King Edward I, often known as 'Edward of Windsor'. A nursery was established for him in the Upper Ward, and two years later, when he needed still more space, Master Simon the carpenter was provided with timber 'for lengthening the chamber of Edward our son'. The birth of the first daughter, Margaret, in September 1240 caused more building so that the children could have their own little courtyard in which to play. The Castle had become a family home – but mainly for the queens consorts and their children. The kings themselves throughout the Middle Ages were constantly on the move – it was not only Elizabeth I who was peripatetic. The itinerary of Edward I suggests that during his reign from 1277 to 1307 he was at Windsor for just a few days each year. Yet these might include

The King of France Miserichord.

memorable occasions for the Castle. In July 1278, for instance, Edward and 35 knights assembled for a splendid tournament in the Park. Account rolls detail the leather-gilt armour, the gilded helms, crests, shields, blunted swords, 800 little bells for the horses' harness, furs from Paris and buckskin gloves provided to equip a 'peaceable joust', intended both as recreation and as military exercise. Jousting of this type developed much further at Windsor under Edward's grandson, Edward III, into something more formal, a 'Round Table' in 1344, and then, in 1348, into the Most Noble Order of the Garter, with its three days of feasts, masses and jousting each year.

As yet, however, Windsor was merely one of several centres of royal life. It was not until 1475 that it acquired some type of dominance. In that year Edward IV began to build a new St George's Chapel which was to contain a grand two-storeyed chantry which would be his burial place. When he died, in 1483, in fact only half the new chapel was completed, but the chantry chapel was there and received his body, also that of his Queen Elizabeth Woodville in 1492, and those of his son George and daughter Margaret. Westminster Abbey, the traditional burial place of monarchs seemed to be replaced by Windsor. However, the Yorkist dynasty was soon extinguished – on the field of Bosworth in 1485 – and the Abbey regained its pre-eminence. Windsor to some extent vied with it, for Henry VIII and

A Drinking Party. This illuminated initial 'O' introduces a Latin drinking song *O potores exquisiti* included in the Windsor Carol Book, a manuscript which was probably made between 1430 and 1444 for St George's Chapel at Windsor Castle.

Charles I are buried at St George's, but only from 1820 onwards was Edward IV's plan adhered to. Members of the Royal Family ever since, after service in St George's, have been buried either in the Chapel, the adjacent Albert Memorial Chapel or in the Royal Mausoleum and its cemetery at nearby Frogmore.

The fact that the mediaeval Castle was both fortress and royal home led to its being in some degree also a centre of government: 'Whitehall', in modern terms, as well as 'Buckingham Palace'. There was a dramatic reminder of this as recently as 1981 when it was necessary to reconstruct the mid-Victorian great west steps of St George's Chapel. Excavations beneath these steps revealed chalk and rubble foundations of an early mediaeval building. Documentary evidence showed that these must have been part of a building known as the Almonry, which in earliest days had been situated elsewhere in the Lower Ward. This office was part of the King's Secretariat or Chancery, presided over by the officer now known as the Lord Chancellor. There were eight clerks whose main job was to redress the wrongs of persons 'of poor estate' who lacked means to sue by the common law. In addition, there was a special Almoner who arranged the annual service and distribution of Maundy Money in Holy Week (which still takes place) and controlled all royal charities. He received the money obtained from the sale of goods of convicted felons that it might be 'given to God in expiation, in order that it might be applied to pious uses'.[6] The drum tower still in the centre of the western castle wall above Thames Street was part of the Almonry quadrangle and was known as the Almoner's Tower, until the whole area passed to the Dean and Canons as part of Edward IV's great re-foundation in 1475.

No other government department seems to have had its permanent headquarters at Windsor. However, since the King intermittently resided there, civil servants, judges and magnates would often be in attendance on him in the Upper Ward (even if they had to lodge in the town). Those royal servants who were clergy, as so many were, sometimes found permanent residence after 1348 in the castle as canons of St George's Chapel. Perhaps the best example was Oliver King, Secretary of State from 1480 to 1483 and again, 1487 to 1500, who probably lived at no. 6 the Cloisters, which was greatly enlarged beyond the size of other canonical lodgings in a manner likely to be fitting for a royal officer of state. Other canons might serve as ambassadors, keepers of the wardrobe, or as masters of the rolls.[7]

This link of the castle with the government of the country cannot be overstressed. It was not simply a mediaeval phenomenon. When I was editing the papers of Sir Edward Dering, M.P., Lord of the Treasury in Charles II's reign from 1679 to 1689, I found that Dering had to come to Windsor frequently. It was here that the then vexed question of how to tax Ireland was discussed;[8] and from that time on, certainly to the end of

Queen Victoria's reign, ministerial discussions frequently took place in the Upper Ward.

Royal residence, governmental centre – not unexpected functions for a royal castle. What was distinctly unusual was that the Castle, and Windsor with it, became a centre of religious pilgrimage. This resulted from Edward III's foundations of 1348. In that year he established the Order of the Garter, and, a parallel body now known as St George's Chapel, a religious house of a semi-monastic type, a 'college of secular canons' to whom he gave Henry III's chapel of 1240 in the Lower Ward, and for whom he erected the elaborate Dean's and Canons' Cloisters with their appertinent Treasury and Chapter House. The only aim expressed in the college's foundation charter was to pray daily for the King, his family, and all faithful departed. But a second, unexpressed, aim was to provide a spiritual home for the Order of the Garter. Stalls were allotted to the Knights in the chapel, over which their banners were placed; and in St George's-tide each year (22 to 25 April) the chapel was the scene of Vespers and Masses for the Order.

The work of Edward III in establishing his college of secular canons has always been recognised as significant for the history of chivalry, of music and of the church. It is only in recent years that we have learned from Dr. John Harvey's two seminal papers in the *Reports of the Friends of St George's* (1961 and 1962) of its significance for architecture. The Dean's Cloister of 1353 is now seen to have been the first example of a collegiate building established round a closed quadrangle. This ground-plan we now take for granted in, for instance, the academic colleges of Oxford and Cambridge. It seems that the ecclesiastical college of Windsor was the innovator in this type of planning.

Secondly, the 1350s were the time when a gothic style unique to England was being developed, a style in which stone tracery, instead of leading sideways into sharply pointed arches and taking up much of the window space, became resolved into uprights and was so thin that walls were composed rather of glass than of stone: the Perpendicular style, in short. John Sponlee's central arcading in the Dean's Cloister is one of the earliest essays in this style (though since extensively remade) and Geoffrey Carlton's contemporary Aerary Porch – still splendidly unspoiled by restoration – is a contrasting and brilliant exercise in the new style. Attention is usually concentrated on the climax of Perpendicular architecture in the 'new' St George's Chapel of 1475–1528, but to architectural historians Edward III's humbler structure of the 1350s is more significant – the most interesting building work in Windsor, castle or borough.

Obviously, members of the public would come to see so splendid a place of worship. But, more important, the Kings gave to the chapel famous

Interior of St George's Chapel.

relics which good Christians would wish to venerate.[9] The first was the largest reputed piece in England of the Cross of Calvary on which Christ was crucified. It had been the property of the Princes of North Wales, and the last Prince, Llewelyn, carried it with him to the battle in 1282 at which he and his cause were lost. The victor, Edward I, appropriated the Cross as spoils of war. It was known as the 'Cross Gneth' (had it once been at Neath in Wales, or had it belonged to a monk called Neotus?) and the King took it on his journeyings, as did his son, Edward II. In about 1332 Edward III gave it to his new college of Windsor after perhaps some £50,000, in our money, had been spent on ornamenting the gold and silver cross in which it was displayed – one workman alone spent as long as two years working on the cross. At the Reformation it was destroyed, but as late as 1503 special priests were in attendance at Windsor on feast days in order to hear the confessions of the crowds who came to adore it. Certainly in its time it was the most famous sacred and valuable object in Windsor.

A Schorn Pilgrim Badge.

But before 1503 the bones of the pious Henry VI, founder of Eton College, together with his spurs, hat and other *personalia*, were alongside the cross. As an embittered reformer later put it, 'The seely bewitched People gathered hither on Pilgrimage, being persuaded that to put upon a Man's Head any olde red Velvet Hatte of his, that laye theare, was a sovereign medicine against the headache'. (But perhaps it was).

Strangest and most popular, in the long run, of all the Windsor relics were the bones of Master John Schorn, a priest of North Marston, Buckinghamshire.[10] At Edward IV's order, in 1478 these were taken and buried in the first part of his new chapel, as a sort of foundation stone of holiness, and, obviously, as an encouragement to pilgrims and their offerings. Schorn had the reputation of being able to heal diseases of the limbs, and a verse described him as 'gentleman born, who conjured the Devil into a boot'. He is often depicted as a preacher in a pulpit, who thrusts the devil by the tail into a long-toed jack-boot. Some think that mechanical models of this type were our first 'Jack-in-the-boxes'.

True Cross; Henry VI; Schorn – idiomatically, these were money-spinners. Schorn's relics alone produced £500 a year in mediaeval currency (very many thousands in ours) for the dean and canons. Foxe records how pilgrims especially from Devon and Cornwall, came 'by plumps', i.e. in vast crowds, to offer at Henry VI's grave, to adore an image of Mary, and so on. Souvenirs, or Windsor 'pilgrim badges', showing Schorn or Henry were on sale in the Castle, and were usually worn in hat bands. Many of them still survive today in the Museum of London, having been lost in the City. Mediaeval Windsor in some sense was a mixture of Walsingham and Lourdes as we know them today.

St George's Chapel as a great place of pilgrimage became not only rather obviously the richest art centre in Windsor, but also the church which, after Westminster Abbey, contains more treasures than any other ecclesiastical building in the whole country. If it is the high point of Windsor's achievement, it is also one of the world's outstanding buildings. So much has been written in guide books and art histories about the chapel that its main features can almost be taken for granted. Perhaps, in conclusion, just two aspects of its rich heritage should be mentioned, each with a national as well as an artistic significance.

First, the iron work. Henry III in 1240 had external doors to the new chapel designed with the most lovely iron scroll work to decorate and strengthen them. These Edward IV maintained as the eastern doors of the 1475 chapel. The iron work is of a superb Romanesque design, flowing elegantly round to a vesica shape inscribed 'Gilebertus' (who was he?). This is 13th century craftsmanship at its highest. Then, guarding Edward IV's tomb of 1483 are iron gates of incredible elaboration and delicacy, with some iron plates paper-thin; still perfect, in almost mint condition, the

View from the Round Tower, by Paul Sandby. Reproduced by gracious permission of Her Majesty the Queen.

finest craftsmanship of the 15th century, and perhaps the best iron work in the country.

Then painting. Looking down on the chantry and tomb of the canon, Bishop Oliver King, is a large and grand oil painting of the 1480s appropriate for what we would now call a great Minister of State. The canon was Secretary in turn to the son of Henry VI, to Edward IV, to Edward V, and to Henry VII and the panel consists of paintings of the four, Edward V (uncrowned and murdered) having the crown shown suspended above his head. Partly painted from the life this is a unique panel; no other contemporary realistic sequence of mediaeval kings is

known. It symbolises several things. Here was, let us say, the Secretary of State or Prime Minister, a canon of Windsor, living in Windsor, buried in Windsor. How inconceivable that our present Prime Minister should live in the Cloisters as a member of the Windsor Chapter. Next, it makes the new status of the Chapel, the Castle and indeed Windsor itself as a national centre, one equally relevant to the Yorkist dynasty and to the Tudor dynasty which displaced it, binding together what we now call mediaeval and modern history. St George's Chapel is not merely great architecture and notable art; as in this painting it symbolises national history both in its revolutions and its (more profound) continuity.

References

1 Unless otherwise indicated, the architectural history outlined in this chapter is based on Hope, 10 – 245, and on incidental references in his second volume, 373 – 587.
2 Shelagh Bond 'The Medieval Constables of Windsor Castle', *English Historical Review*, lxxxii (1967), 225 – 249.
3 P. Warner, *The Medieval Castle* (1971), 45.
4 Hope, 23 – 4.
5 ibid. 26 – 8.
6 Mark Burch and Maurice Bond 'The Western Steps of St George's Chapel: An Historical and Archaeological Report', RF St G (1981 – 2). 98 – 108.
7 S.L. Ollard 'The Deans and Canons of Windsor' (M St GC) (1950), especially lists on 162 – 3. On the general history of the mediaeval Chapel see M St GC: A.K.B. Roberts, 'St George's Chapel, Windsor Castle 1348 – 1416' (1947); the introduction by M.F. Bond to J. Dalton, 'The Manuscripts of St George's Chapel' (1957), and the introduction to S. Bond, 'The Chapter Acts of the Dean and Canons of Windsor' (1966), together with very many specialist articles in RF St G.
8 Maurice Bond, *The diaries and papers of Sir Edward Dering* (1976), 127 – 8, 131, 149.
9 On relics at Windsor, see W. Coombe Tennant, 'Croes Naid', RF St G (1943), 8; Maurice Bond, *The Inventories of St George's Chapel*, (1947), 279 – 287; Brian Spencer, 'King Henry of Windsor and the London Pilgrim', *Collectanea Londoniensia* (1978), 235 – 264; and the forthcoming note on a King Henry VI Book of Hours in RF St G (1972 – 3). For Schorn, see note below.
10 Two articles, by R.T. Pelly and Maurice Bond respectively, are in RF St G (1949), 18 – 27, with additional information by Canon Derek Eastman in RF St G (1979 – 80), 19 – 22.

The Mediaeval Town

None of this could have happened without the town. The castle and the chapel depended on the town for supplies, for extra accommodation, and for personal service. But whilst it is fairly easy to visualise the mediaeval castle – its main structure is still profoundly of the Middle Ages – the town is less evocative of its past, and particularly of its mediaeval past. One of its main shopping streets is a typical suburban jumble of 20th century chain-stores and dress shops; the Victorian age had previously laid its hand heavily on the town; and post-1946 town development plans, whilst removing slums and preventing 'inner-city blight', have installed an almost overwhelming number of offices for multi-national companies needing quick access to the M4, only a mile away, and Heathrow airport.

But Windsor's history is not quite so hidden as it might at first sight appear. We have two aids. Firstly, the actual street plan of inner Windsor today is that of Henry III's time and although none of its buildings date back to that reign except for the superlative church of St Andrew at Clewer (which is in fact mainly Norman), a good number of timber-framed structures are today easily recognisable in the centre of the town. Moreover, we have an excellent guide to mediaeval and Tudor Windsor, because in 1607 John Norden, the great cartographer, made for James I a survey of 'the Honour of Windsor' which included a bird's-eye view of the town. The appropriate part of this survey, illustrated here, is our starting point.[1]

Norden shows just over 180 buildings – although he cuts Peascod Street short at the right hand margin of his map, and so omits another dozen or so before the 'Town's end'. Not it seems, a large town; but very few mediaeval towns were in fact large. Rome itself in the later Middle Ages had only 17,000 inhabitants and Windsor (without neighbouring Clewer) probably had a thousand or so, though doubling this when pilgrimages and court residences attracted the world to Windsor.

There are essentially two streets, on which the town is still threaded. These appear clearly both in Norden's Survey and also in Dr. Astill's recent plan of Windsor's mediaeval features. They are the main highway from the bridge over the Thames running south to the parkland, now known successively as Thames Street, High Street and Park Street. Then, forming a T-junction with it in the centre, is the street cut short by Norden, Peascod Street, which goes westwards to the forest. Let us start in the bottom right-hand corner of Norden's map, at the north end of Windsor, with 'Windesore Bridge'. This he shows as a wooden structure, apparently of three arches. In fact it had a dozen or more until it was completely replaced

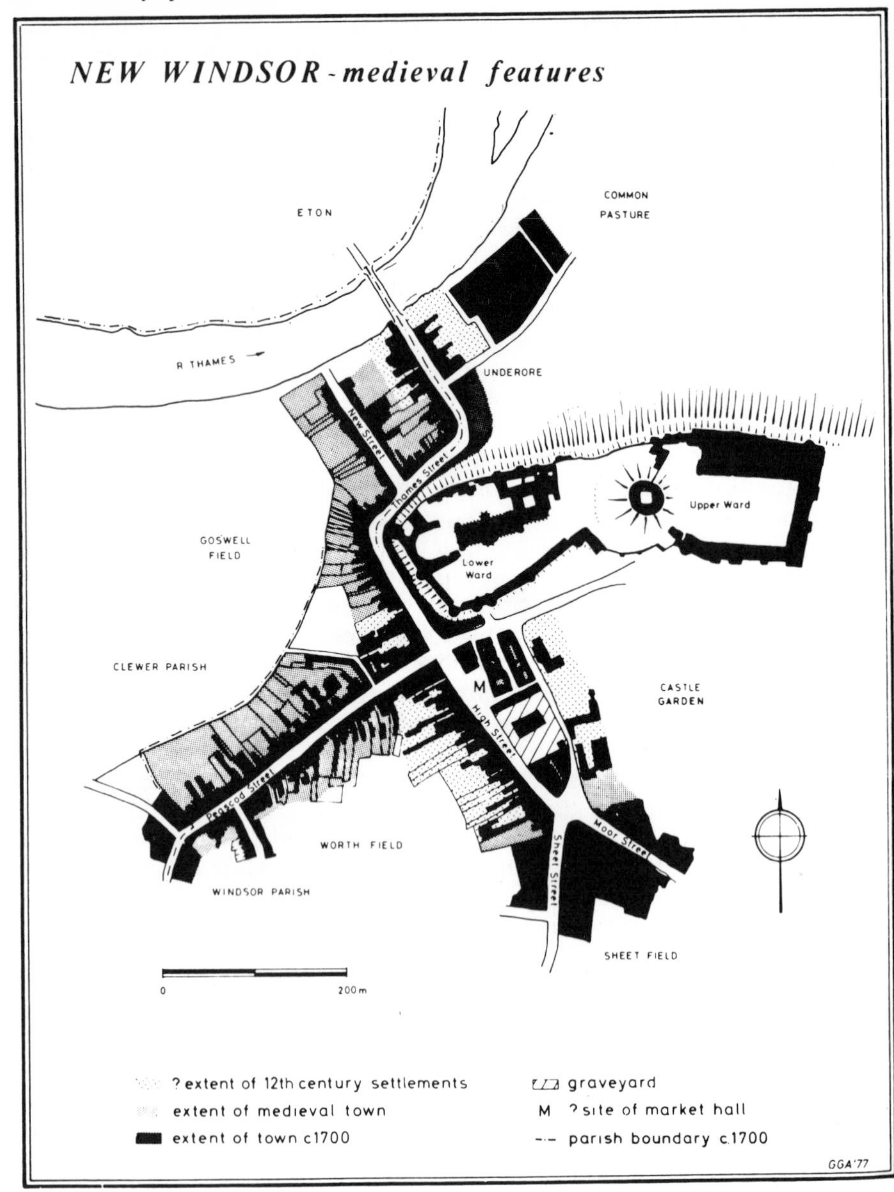

Dr Astill's diagram showing the extent of the mediaeval town.

in 1822 by the present iron bridge. First mentioned in 1236, when five oaks were granted for its repair, this bridge was vital to both borough and castle as a link with London. To secure its maintenance the town had the right to collect tolls from those passing over it – which it continued to do until this century – and also from those sailing under it (these tolls were known as pontage). Eustace Harwood in *Windsor Old and New* reminds us that the bridge was such an expense that in 1551 the Borough chamberlain or treasurer sold two silver chalices in order to raise £15 for its repair.[2]

Norden sketches in three craft, two with oars, one with a sail, navigating the bridge, and there is a broad tow-path on the Windsor side. Stow, a few years earlier in 1598, had written of two thousand wherries and small boats habitually using the Thames, and, from the Middle Ages, barges were also to be seen, hauled by horses led along the tow-path. The tow-ropes were troublesome to Windsor people as they were pulled right across the road at the bridge, but so were the large number of horses; often one barge might need twelve horses to draw it against the current. Kings travelled to Windsor by barge from London; stone for work at the Castle came downstream from Oxford and upstream from Caen in Normandy;[3] timber was moved in great quantities. The wharf-side by the bridge was Windsor's front-door; Windsor was pre-eminently a river-port, as in its earliest days Saxon Windsor had been, the place where goods were lifted to the bank with a windlass.

From the river, Norden shows Thames Street winding up round the edge of the original cliff at Clewer hill and the 1230 western wall of the castle to the centre of the town, where he writes 'windesore' – passing the lane to Datchet on the left, and on the right a road which has been successively New street, Bier street (along which coffins may have been carried to Clewer church), and, now, River Street. A rail on the right of Thames Street protects pedestrians from the traffic and helps them up the steep slope, and at the top of the hill two inn-signs are shown. Some of the timber-frame houses can still be seen: the earliest, the *Swan* and, opposite to it, the *William IV,* the former perhaps dating back to the 1500s. In a recently formed courtyard half-way up the hill can be seen a shop perhaps dating back to the 1400s. Other brick or plaster facades hide inner structures of the 17th century.

But the most obvious links with the past are the cobbled streets, shown, not very accurately by Norden, between the castle and the church, west of an early market house standing on stilts which is now gone. The picturesque complex of Market Street, Church Street, St Alban's Street, and, at right angles, Church Lane represent the original twelfth century planning of a town at the gate of the castle, the first settlement of traders coming from Old Windsor. The units within this area today are still small, squarish, and practically without gardens. On Castle Hill at the castle side of this block are nos. 4 (The Horse and Groom) and nos. 10 and 11, all timber-framed of about Norden's time. Then no. 7 Church Street and, at its end, nos. 9 – 12, are very visibly early buildings, the last with typical overhanging first storey. Finally, in Church Lane at no. 4 there is today a fine four floor timber structure, disguised by plastering, which was certainly a century or two old in Norden's day.

Norden shows the stocks, in High Street, just beyond the Market House, but he does not include the ultimate deterrent, the gallows. These stood in the continuation of High Street, where it swings to the left, nowadays known as Park Street. It led to Frogmore and was first called Moor Street, then, as it had the town pound for stray animals, it changed its name to Pound Street, before becoming Park Street in the 18th century.

The truncated road on Norden's plan to the right from the Market House was originally an enclosure where peas were grown, then a way through it became Peascroft street, now Peascod (pronounced Pescot) Street. By Norden's time clearly nothing was grown there. He shows a solid line of houses on both sides with their own crofts behind. Modernised as the street now is, it still contains some Norden-type houses, certainly no. 140, near the top on the south side, and no. 27, lower down, on the south side. In all, probably about 28 of the 180 buildings in Norden's map of 1607 can be identified; and incidental features, often the basements of other properties date back to his century. Norden's – and Shakespeare's – Windsor is not wholly lost.

These timber-framed buildings, however, were not themselves original. They represented replacements by the wealthy of much simpler buildings. At Windsor, as elsewhere, domestic building seems to have gone through three stages.[4] The earliest was that in which buildings were of unbaked earth or cob walls with thatched roofs and earth floors. Then came the half-timbered buildings of the later Middle Ages. Timber at Windsor obviously was plentiful and it must have been needed in quantity. For the mid-14th century works at the castle 3,000 oaks had to be cut down, and an average timber-framed farm house might need up to 35 trees. But although relatively cheap, these houses were frequently being burn down, and brick, which had begun as a filling for the timber frames became, after 1660, at Windsor as elsewhere, the fashionable material for a town. Again, Windsor was lucky. Just as it had oak trees in abundance, it also had good London clays, excellent for brick-making. Until metal and concrete appeared in recent centuries Windsor building was highly 'vernacular'.

One feature of Windsor's life before 1700 is not clearly indicated by Norden. Windsor was in part a farming community. Most Windsor houses were backed, as he indicates, by small gardens or crofts, but behind them were open fields. One of these, the Worth, is shown as an empty space to the right of High Street. Both the Saxon village of Clewer and the Norman

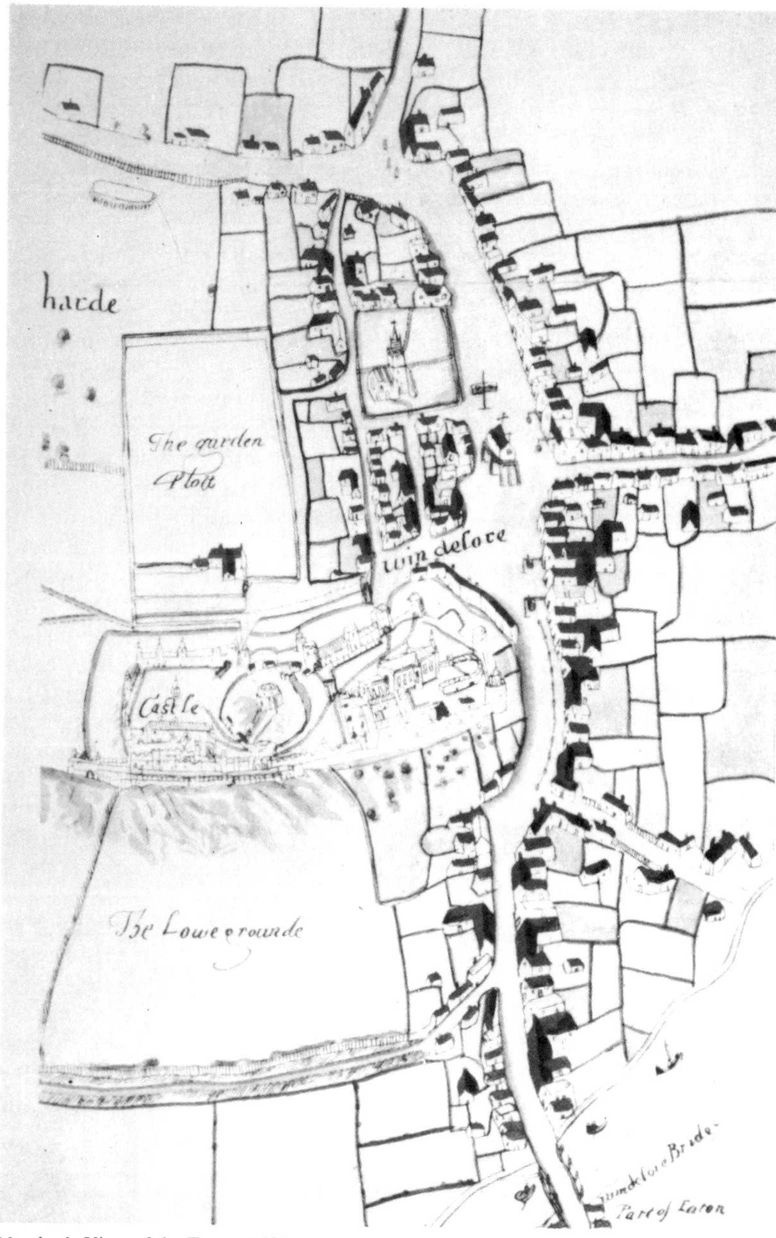

Norden's View of the Town, 1607.

town of New Windsor had some type of open field system by which inhabitants owned individual strips scattered in large open fields.[5] These are the fields across which Mine Host of the Garter in Shakespeare's *Merry Wives* sends the doctor to his rendezvous in Frogmore. There were three main fields for New Windsor, used for the growth of oats or wheat. The Worth lay between Peascod Street and Sheet Street; the Sheet was to its east, stretching across what is now the Long Walk; and then, where the Royal Gardens now are, on the way to Old Windsor, was High Field, with a smaller field, 'Spelters' on the Old Windsor boundary. By Norden's time a process of enclosure had consolidated individual holdings in the Sheet and the Worth – Norden clearly marks 7 enclosures round the shrunken Worth, and the Sheet is called 'Parte of Cresswells walke' and contains a dozen or so enclosures. However, as late as 1697 the more distant fields, Highfield and Spelters, still had long narrow strips in them. William Biggs, for instance, was cultivating a strip in Highfield of precisely one acre, about 480 yards long and 10 yards wide. To the south he had two more (separated) strips respectively of ½ acre and 1 acre; to the north, two more strips, which suffered from being cut in half by Gallows Lane running diagonally across them.[6]

Windsor combined arable farming with stock. There was extensive meadow land, beginning with the Goosefields (to become notorious later as the slums known as the Goswells), which lay along the river side behind Peascod Street. Where Norden shows 'The Lowe grounde', 'Litle Parke' etc. had been in earlier centuries more meadows and grazing land for Windsor – much of it known as Datchet Mead. Here there was a right for the burgesses of Windsor to pasture sheep and cattle all the year round. After Lammas day in August, cattle could be turned out also to pasture on arable lands, on condition (in 1610) that each landowner for every acre of meadow held could pasture one cow, and for every three acres of arable, another cow. These rights of common also extended to other outlying fields such as Spital Hill, Hog Common and Frogmore Fields.

Historic Windsor thus was to some extent a farming community, and perhaps its country aspect is best conveyed in an engraving by Hoefnagel showing a shepherd drowsily watching his flock of sheep in the fields near Datchet Lane; roughly on the site of what is still called Farmyard and the neighbouring Riverside railway station. And although post-mediaeval Windsor was hardly an agricultural centre, even in the 1740s one of the three annual Fairs (at St John Baptist's-tide on 24th June) was for the buying and selling of Wool.

In considering Norden's map, one town building has not yet been mentioned: the most important, in stone and not timber, and centrally situated – the parish church of St John Baptist. It is a commonplace that the mediaeval parish church was normally both the religious and the social

Clewer Map.

centre of community life. In Windsor there was the slight complexity that part of the town lay in the more ancient parish of Clewer. Some of the parishioners from Peascod and Thames Streets would therefore have to take footpaths across the Goswells to the parish church of St Andrew. This, as we have seen, still stands, after a major Victorian restoration, in Clewer village and on the banks of the river. Windsor's Norman church with sundry rebuildings became unsafe, and was completely replaced by a new structure in 1822. But although some bays longer, the old church seems to have been very much a twin of what we can still see at Clewer; so the best way to realise physically the town's own central building is to visit St Andrew at Clewer, and there admire the Romanesque arches, the deeply splayed windows, the flint and clunch walls, the superb Norman (or Saxon?) font, together with the various 13th and 14th century developments which make it externally look a Gothic rather than a Norman church.[7]

Clewer had a great benefactor in Sir Bernard de Brocas in the 14th century; Windsor had no such benefactor, but with its commanding position in the town it had the support of the ruling fraternity and the various guilds of the merchants, and was clearly prosperous.

The first mention of the Windsor church was in 1184,[8] when, along with Old Windsor church, it was given as an endowment to the Austin Canons of Waltham Abbey, who thus became Rectors, with the duties of maintaining the chancels of the churches and of nominating substitutes, i.e. 'vicars' for themselves in order to care for the parish. As Rector, the Abbey received all revenues from parishioners due to a Rector, such as the taxes, or tithes, on animals owned by each parishioner, agricultural produce annually acquired and profits from private trading. Eventually the system was that the Abbot of Waltham received hundreds of pounds a year from the people of Windsor to cover all this, and the rest, about £15, largely went towards paying the vicar's stipend and to church maintenance. Windsor vicars in fact became quite wealthy men, and in 1358 William Mere, vicar, was able to purchase 80 acres of arable meadow and woodland in Windsor – vicars were, of course, farmers as well as priests, and their High Street vicarage would have looked somewhat like a farmhouse. The Clewer rector was a resident priest and had his own vast tithe barn in which to store the rector's tithes (which of course did not have to go to a far away monastery), and was equally a wealthy man.

Under the Windsor vicar and the Clewer rector were junior, very junior, clergy, licensed chaplains, hired priests, deacons and acolytes, who besides assisting in church, might help in educational work, and perhaps also work on the farm.

Within the parish of Windsor was one ecclesiastical and royal foundation that lived its own independent life: the leper hospital, founded in 1168 (by

Henry II, it would seem). This was dedicated to St Peter, and presided over by a priest-chaplain nominated by the king. It is likely that the main buildings, a hall and a chapel, were situated in St Leonard's Road. After a century it expanded, being given by Henry III 120 acres taken from the Forest – this must have been the area stretching from Bolton Road to Stag Meadow. Lacking, unusually, convents or friaries, this was Windsor's only religious house, and it did not last into the modern period. By the 15th century leprosy itself had almost been conquered, and just as tuberculosis sanatoria in Switzerland have been converted into hotels, other uses were found for leprosana.

St Peter's Hospital was given in 1462 by Edward IV to Eton College, and the extensive properties became a source of income for the College. In the 19th century some of the meadows became brickfields and what is now Bolton Crescent was an area of clay pits, which became ponds and eventually serving as bottle dumps for the mineral water factory on the site of the leper hospital itself. (Clarence Crescent was, in a sense, built out of the future Bolton Crescent). Mediaeval buildings do not survive, but the name 'Spital' is in general use for that part of Windsor, stretching, coincidentally, from the new King Edward VII Hospital in St Leonard's Road southwards to St Agnes Church.

Parishioners would have kept well away from St Peter's Hospital, but life in the town must have revolved round the two parish churches.

Within the churches the dominant feature would not be, as it is today, a high altar or the Reserved Sacrament, but a sequence of side altars, at St John's Windsor perhaps corresponding to the eight bays and windows on each side. Each altar was dedicated to a particular saint and would have its own flickering altar light. An inventory of 1226 indicates which saints were favoured by Windsor. On a normal Sunday 22d was collected from the congregation, but on the patron saint's day, St John Baptist, as much as 15 shillings, and on St Nicholas' day, 2 shillings. By 1426 there were 13 named lights maintained over the altars, really a series of sub-churches, each with its own vestments and altar plate and sometimes its own priest. Each was a centre of devotion for some group of townspeople. In particular, the altar of the Holy Trinity became linked with the governing corporation, and in the early 1500s was given to two Wardens to supervise. The Trinity Guild so formed held property and paid for the most elaborate funerals and commemorative services for its brothers and sisters.

On Sundays and Saints' days Windsor people went to their appropriate church, but not necessarily much further than the churchyard. St Bernardino in a famous sermon in Siena gives a good picture of a Sunday morning when he tells his hearers not to stay outside in the porch, talking about their oxen and the amount of land they have ploughed and just rushing in to church at the moment of the elevation of the host. Yet the church, whether at Siena or in Windsor, was the single most important feature in parishioners' life, not only before the Reformation but for some time afterwards. The pattern of their day was set by the bells of the church. No work was done on saints' days. Eating was regulated by the church – in 1400 Wednesdays, Fridays and Saturdays only produced salt fish for the humble – and in Lent eggs as well as meat were prohibited. Brighter children were taken to one of the minor clergy to be taught reading and writing; and indeed for poorer townspeople further education and ordination were the only way to escape from the customary life of a servant or labourer. In Windsor and other towns apprenticeship to a craft or trade was an additional alternative for a few, but here also elementary education had to be sought from the clergy, or after the Reformation, from 'dames' or other private enterprise. When a larger and more formal school was founded in Windsor in 1710 it became the foundation of a developing and important system of church schools.

Norden included one church in his plan, even if his survey did not extend far enough westwards to include the other. A more striking omission is that of shops. There are inns (always plentiful in a fortress and garrison town) and at one point, barrels, to represent Windsor's only industry; but the rest of the buildings seem to be private houses. There are no apparent shops. This is absolutely right. As one walked up the hill from the bridge the

The Seal of the mediaeval Borough of Windsor.

buildings in Thames Street and High Street would have looked like a series of private houses (as several still were in High Street in the 1920s). Although some houses certainly functioned as shops the main shops were the market stalls to which goods were taken for sale on market days (eventually Saturdays only) and which were set up in the wide High Street, starting at the Market House and then stretching along to Pound Street. Some traders visited Windsor's market from a distance; tolls from trading on market days and fees for setting up stalls amounted to such sums as £15 in the year. A certain localisation of trade, as well as a breakaway from rigid market controls is suggested by the existence of 'Drapery Row', where the Guildhall now is; Butchers' Row, now Market Street; and Fish Street, now Church Street; but all of these are adjacent to the Market House and represent a localisation which in the case of fish and of meat was probably both useful and hygienic. Then, in addition there were the annual fair days[9] twice a year, on the vigils of St George, patron saint of the Chapel, and St John Baptist, patron saint of the town (i.e. 22 April and 23 June though for 22 April was later substituted 13 October, the feast of St Edward the Confessor), but then lasting four or five days. Tolls again were payable by those setting up stalls and a tight control was maintained over all forms of trading then as on market days. Until the 18th century the concept of a general freedom to make goods, or to trade in them, was resisted. Windsor was essentially a community of merchants who by their own apprenticeship and skill had a right to trade; they were not going to allow others to invade these rights without making due payment.

Norden has shown us what Windsor looked like. The two churches have hinted at ways in which some aspects of townspeoples' lives were controlled. There remains 'local government', not only the control of trading, but the maintenance of law and order, the enforcement of national laws, and the making of local regulations or by-laws. Windsor as a borough was one of many hundreds in the country, but as historians have found out to their cost, each borough has been slightly different from its neighbour, even when its initial charter gave it rights and privileges according to the customs of another town, and over centuries by-laws and unchallenged custom gave special identity to each urban community.[10]

The starting point for Windsor is its emergence from immediate dependence on the Crown and royal bailiffs by the grant of a charter of freedom. This came on 28 May 1277 when New Windsor became a free borough (*liber burgus*), authorised to have, or to continue to have (we do not know which) a guild of merchants to undertake the supervision of what we have been discussing, the crafts and trade of the town. The charter relieved the inhabitants of a royal tax on pigs. It also made Windsor the place where the King's Justices were to hold court and where county prisoners were to be gaoled. This last provision in some sense made

Windsor the county town of Berkshire, but its position at the extreme east of the county was awkward, and was probably the reason why the gaol was shifted to Wallingford by 1359. Soon after the grant of the charter in 1277, the men of Windsor were also given the right 'to hold the borough to farm for ever', that is, one communal payment or 'farm' to the King each year freed its inhabitants from individual payments. In addition, this ended the supervision of Windsor by royal bailiffs and enabled the borough to elect its own. The list of known bailiffs begins in 1299 with Edmund de Brumpton and Henry le Ledeyetere, and continued into the modern period. These bailiffs, themselves Windsor inhabitants, collected the local dues which then enabled them to pay the fee farm, usually £17 a year. The bailiffs had custody of all prisoners, and they presided over the Borough court of justice.

A dual leadership is an awkward thing. Soon the bailiffs were joined, and, in fact, dominated by a new officer; in 1336 he was called the 'Steward of the Gild' – one might class this as the chairman of the guild or company of Windsor merchants. Then, in 1363, John Peyntour is described as a 'greater person'; in latin *maior*, for us, the Mayor of the Borough. The same individual then seems often to have been both Steward and Mayor, but after 1439 the title of Steward does not appear, and Mayors of New Windsor reigned supreme from Ralph Chippys in 1439 to John Procter in 1974. The Mayors were elected annually at the same time as the Bailiffs, and as mayors they received letters and writs from the kings, served as coroners, and as clerks of the Borough Court, had wills proved before them, and supervised the transfer of lands by 'final concords'. The court, under the Mayor and two Bailiffs, sat every three weeks in the hall of the Guild, with 'power and authority to hear and determine pleas concerning lands, tenements and other matters concerning the Borough'.[11]

This court dealt with law suits. But Windsor was directly administered by what we now think of as a town council – originally at Windsor, the 'fraternity' or brotherhood. There were not more than 30 members, but with special groups within them, e.g. 7 aldermen; 6 benchers; other burgesses; and, most junior, the brethren. All must be freemen of the borough who had served their apprenticeship and had then been made 'free' of the guild with the right to exercise a craft or trade. Service was for life; admission to the fraternity was by co-option; attendance at meetings was compulsory under fine. As Shelagh Bond has said, this was an exclusive and select club which preserved its dominance for some five centuries, sometimes, as for instance, in the 17th century, seeking to limit to themselves the right to vote in parliamentary elections.

From time to time the fraternity made by-laws for the better government of the town. One such law dates from 1377, with a quite full code in 1474, amended in 1499 and 1580. Many by-laws prescribed with almost Venetian complexity how the fraternity should function. A key by-law of 1474 empowered the Mayor or his deputy, an Alderman, 'to take and carry to the stocks or prison any person being a peace breaker, fighter, quarreler, scolder, or any other misdemeaned person'. In general, however, the fraternity were mostly concerned with the control of trade – as we have suggested, there was no free-market in the fourteenth and fifteenth centuries. After apprenticeship, fines were levied for admission to freedom. These varied considerably. A chandler paid £30 4s 1d in 1687; the next year a somewhat humbler tallow-chandler, only 3s 4d, 'in respect he had long been in the town.' Women could become free; together with their men colleagues they paid (in 1683) a quarterly sum to the common chest of the fraternity. The first *Hall Book* shows the fraternity busily prohibiting the colouring of wares by foreigners, i.e. non-freemen, and rigidly defining where in Windsor vegetables, horses, cows and fish could be sold. The fraternity was all-seeing.

The composition of the oligarchy gives a good idea of which trades were carried on in Windsor, or at least, of which led to high office. Between 1653 and 1725, of 50 Mayors, 13 were providers of food – cheesemongers, butchers, confectioners, fishmongers, bakers and grocers; 7 were craftsmen – armourer, clock-maker, blacksmith, painter-stainer, carpenter, glazier and goldsmith. And an important five helped to provide Windsor with ale and wine.[12] The leading burgesses were thus men providing services. Only one was concerned with farming (other than as a side-line), and only 19 out of 326 admitted to the freedom were farmers or rivermen. Windsor from being part agricultural, part mercantile, had become a predominantly mercantile and craft community.

This reflects the sociology of mediaeval and early modern Windsor. And its sociology is very largely its history – as it is for most small communities of a thousand or two. But Windsor served a castle and one of the main themes of this book is the extent, varying from century to century, to which the town was caught up in the life of the castle and, further, of the nation. Two of the earliest and harshest events have been mentioned: the sieges of 1193 and 1216. In 1277 Windsor got its charter; in 1302 it sent its first known representatives to Parliament. Then came a tragedy, followed by an almost compensatory stimulus. In 1349 the outbreak of the Black Death led to the possible death of something like a third of Windsor's population. We do not have direct figures, but there is no reason to think the town was exempt from the general mortality, and we know that the plague brought to a complete halt major building work in the Castle. But then, from 1350 to at least 1365, large groups of workmen came to Windsor to carry out Edward III's elaborate building projects, for the canons in the Lower Ward and for the royal family in the Upper Ward. In some years it is possible that up to 485 masons and 1,483 labourers were working in the Castle, for varying periods of time, ranging from 11 days to 144 days in the accounting year.[13] The coming of a thousand or more workmen to Windsor must have made enormous calls on the Windsor tradesmen for supplies, even if the men camped out in the Castle precincts.

Building in the Castle then came somewhat to a stop; though the poet Geoffrey Chaucer makes an appearance as Clerk of the Works when St George's Chapel needed repair in Richard II's reign. And Windsor, like in fact many other mediaeval towns, seemed to go into some sort of decline. In 1439 an enquiry revealed that Windsor 'by great mortality and pestilence at various times, was emptied and wasted', its inhabitants were moneyless.[14] King Henry VI accepted this as fact, and reduced the borough rent from £17 to £10 a year. To encourage civic life further Henry VI gave the borough wider, exclusive civil and criminal jurisdiction (with its accompanying fines) together with freedom from its freemen having to pay dues such as pontage and stallage elsewhere in England.

The mid 15th century was not, however, wholly beneficial to Windsor. The Crown perhaps felt shut in by the borough. The castle was surrounded by Windsor's fields and meadows, which had to be crossed before courtiers hawking and hunting could reach the royal forest areas. Edward IV therefore in the 1460s 'emparked' 200 acres on the east of the Castle, where until then Windsor's farm animals had pastured and where flint and chalk had been freely dug. No doubt in recompense, a Charter was issued in 1466 continuing the reduced rent of £10 and making the borough a corporation with the right to sue and be sued and possessing its own common seal – which spelt full burghal autonomy as mediaeval England knew it.[15]

Then, once more, the fortunes of Windsor were improved by a royal building programme. Under King Edward IV, the new St George's Chapel between 1475 and 1483 (continued again, 1503 – 9) involved the bringing of stone, timber, gravel, sand and lime to Windsor wharfside and the provisioning of what must once more have been some thousand or so masons, carpenters, carvers, sawyers, smiths, tilers, labourers and others.[16] Then, as the chapel was built, the shrines and altars began to attract hundreds of pilgrims. The poverty of 1439 gives way to what as we shall see may be considered relative wealth in the early Tudor period; royal residence and holy relics between them had given Windsor a new lease of life.

A vivid reminder of what royal residence meant to Windsor comes with a detailed description of the visit of Philip, King of Castile, to King Henry VII in 1506.[17] This was an event of national importance, although it resulted from pure accident. Philip, having won victory in a war in the Low Countries was sailing home to Spain when his ships were driven by gales on to the coast of Dorset. Somewhat rashly, and certainly spontaneously, he decided to land and visit King Henry VII. Henry, who had been seeking

A view of Thames Street and the town taken from the Castle.

some sort of diplomatic initiative for himself, sent instructions for all gentry on the route from Dorset to Windsor (where he then was) to help Philip on his way, and palfreys and litters were sent to speed the journey. On 31 January the Prince of Wales (later King Henry VIII) with five earls and 500 others 'gorgeously apparelled' rode five miles out of Windsor, it would seem to a field or open woodland in Winkfield, in order to meet Philip and accompany him to 'an arable field' which was 'a mile or more out of Windsor', perhaps our present Clewer Green. There Henry VII awaited them. The Kings met, embraced, and then rode in procession to the Castle, up Peascod Street and Castle Hill. At the main Castle Gateway (not yet 'Henry VIII's Gateway'), with the Officers of Arms bearing their arms, trumpets blowing, the Sword of State was carried into the Castle by the Earl of Derby before the two Kings.

During nearly a fortnight Philip remained at the Castle, entertained by dancing, feasting and hunting. But there was more to it than festivities. Philip was made a Knight of the Garter, and a treaty was discussed and then agreed before the High Altar of the new Chapel,[18] in which England and Castile bound themselves by a strict union of alliance. Philip signed on behalf of his father, the Holy Roman Emperor. At a final banquet Henry VII said 'You have seen the Round Table at Winchester of which so much has been said and written; but I hope that in future men will talk of this table at which a perpetual friendship was made between the Empire of Rome, the Kingdom of Castile, Flanders and Brabant, and the Kingdom of England.' The Treaty of Windsor, for so it is generally known, was not perpetual – as the Spanish Armada of 1588 demonstrated – but in its day it had significance, and, for us, it shows Windsor as a focal point. The royal cavalcade riding through the streets of Windsor represents some hundreds of state visits subsequently paid to Sovereigns at Windsor, of which that of President Reagan in 1982 is the most recent, helicopters replacing palfreys.

The Treaty of Windsor in some sense ended an epoch. It was sealed by the first of the new Tudor dynasty; it just preceded the coming of ideas summarised by historians as the Reformation and the Renaissance. For Windsor the mediaeval town plan and the mediaeval system of government continued to the 19th century; but by the 1500s Windsor was starting to change the character of its life as it reacted to new governmental methods and also to an overwhelming religious revolution.

References

1 TD reproduce those parts of the Survey dealing with the Castle, the Forest, and the Little Park (including the town) from the original version in the British Library, Harleian MS 3749.

2 Harwood provides valuable detail of the history of the bridge, 7, 8, 10 etc.

3 Hope 107ff.

4 See L.F. Cave, *The Smaller English House* (1981), passim.

5 The best representation of these strips in common fields is in the 1717 estate maps of Clewer, recently discovered by an itinerant butcher (who was interested in local history) in a local dustbin, and by him presented to BRO.

6 The very rare folio edition of TD includes a reproduction of a 1697 survey of Shaw and Frogmore showing these strips in Windsor common fields.
7 Harwood makes frequent mention of the church at Clewer; the Brocas chantry at Clewer is noted in M. Burrows, *The Family of Brocas of Beaurepaire* (1886) 80, 119 – 122, 198; there is an illustrated guide, *The Parish Church of St Andrew, Clewer, Windsor* by Joan A. Hewitt (1972); Sir Nikolaus Pevsner provides a succinct description in *Berkshire* (1966), 308; and the Rector of Clewer maintains an extremely interesting exhibition concerning both the Church and the Parish in the Church Lodge. See also VCH iii (1923), 74 – 76, which has a dated ground plan.
8 Similar references apply to the Windsor Church; Harwood, 337 – 348; VCH iii, 66 – 69, though with no plan; Pevsner, 298 – 9; the current edition of the Guide to the Church; and, again, a helpful exhibition this time in the western vestibules. On the Leper Hospital, see VCH, ii, 101 – 2.
9 Harwood, 111 – 2, etc.
10 The definitive study of Windsor's constitution (on which the following paragraphs are based) is that of Shelagh Bond in her 'The Medieval Constitution of New Windsor' BAJ, vol 65, 21 – 39, supplemented by her introduction to *The First Hall Book . . . 1653 – 1725* (1968), xii – xvi. The surviving original Charters are preserved in BRO.
11 One mediaeval Court Roll survives for 1470 – 1480, in BRO.
12 S. Bond, *The First Hall Book*, xi – xii.
13 Hope, chapter 11.
14 TD, i, 305 – 311, which include the text of the consequent charter of 19 May 1439.
15 Ibid, 361 – 3.
16 See Hope, chapters 21 – 22.
17 TD, i, 434 – 444.
18 Rena Gardiner has reconstructed the scene in the Chapel in her lithograph *The Story of St George's Chapel, Windsor Castle* (1981), 20 – 21.

Tudor and Stuart Windsor

In the mid-fifteenth century Windsor had become 'emptied and wasted'. Various indicators show the remarkable turn-around in the sixteenth century. Windsor under the Tudors was one of the richer towns of the realm. In terms of the tax or subsidy paid by residents to the Crown, Windsor comes thirty-second in the country. A few towns were very wealthy: at the top of the league Norwich, paying £1,704 in the 1520s, and Bristol, £1,072. But many important towns paid at lower levels; Cambridge, £181; Northampton, £180; Plymouth, £163; and Winchester, £132. Amongst this group of notable towns Windsor stands quite proudly (if reluctantly) with its £178.[1] This perhaps, in the early 1500s, was the high point in Windsor's history so far as competing wth other towns is concerned. In 1334 Windsor on a tax quota had come well below 42 other English towns; and, in 1662, on hearth tax payments, Windsor had sunk further to 44th, having within its boundaries (at a slightly earlier date, in 1610) some 1,368 taxed hearths, as against 1,610 in Northampton, and about 2,600 in Plymouth. So under the Tudors Windsor was relatively well-to-do for a small community of a thousand or so.[2]

The reasons are not obscure. The Castle was still a favoured royal residence. To it crowds of nobles and courtiers came – in 1519 there were so many that each nobleman according to his degree was restricted to a certain number of horses 'in consideration of a scarcity and straitness of lodgings'. A Duke could only bring some 60 horses to Windsor, a Marquess, 50, and so on down the social scale.[3]

Processions to the Castle took in a still wider area than that for Philip of Castile. On Garter day in 1520 Henry VIII rode from the Castle to Colnbrook, and with a cavalcade of some 300 horses, then went into procession through Upton to Eton College 'where all they of the College stood along', and over the bridge to a field 'at the Town's end' (presumably in Datchet Lane) where stood Queen Katharine of Aragon and her ladies. Up Thames Street for a solemn reception by the Dean and Canons at the main gateway, before the celebration of the first of the Garter services in St George's Chapel.[4]

When, a generation later, in 1554, Queen Mary married King Philip of Spain in Winchester Cathedral, they then came, so to speak, for a honeymoon, to Windsor. There, approaching as the earlier Philip of Castile had, from the south, they were met at the lower end of Peascod Street by the Mayor and Corporation, 'and thence, the trumpets sounding, they proceeded with the officers of arms before them', up Peascod Street to St George's Chapel, where King Philip was installed Knight of the Garter.[5]

Crispe's Optician's shop, Peascod Street in the 1920s, showing the typical Tudor overhang.

But the mention of Mary, 'Bloody Mary' in fact, is a reminder that the Tudor period was not all pageantry and peace. Windsor did not escape some of the worst of religious strife; it experienced martyrdoms, and came near to the third siege in its history.

In 1534 King and Parliament repudiated papal authority. By that year Windsor had its Protestant groups, even within St George's Chapel. On one occasion, when the choir was singing an anthem to Mary, hailing her as redeemer and saviour ('O redemptrix et salvatrix') some of the Lay Clerks, who were reformers, sang back 'Non redemptrix nec salvatrix' (neither redeemer nor saviour). Foxe comments that 'so striving there with O and Non who should have the mastery, they made an end of the verse. Whereat was good laughing in the sleeves of some.'[6]

But the religious divisions were not a laughing matter, and were not confined to the choir of St George's. In 1536 a priest and a butcher were hanged for treasonable Protestant views in Windsor. A little later in that year, the new Vicar of Windsor, Thomas Melster, once a friar, began preaching ultra-Catholic sermons.[7] A churchwarden, Henry Filmer, with a group of laymen, first persuaded the vicar to keep to central Catholic doctrines and not talk about 'Marian miracles'. But a lawyer, William Simons, felt this was not enough, and starting making notes of the vicar's sermons in St John's parish church. Filmer and Simons then led rival deputations from Windsor to Bishop Capon of Salisbury, and the vicar went along also, as Foxe comments 'which was a painful journey for the silly poor man, by reason he had a sore leg'. Filmer got there first as a result, and easily won over the bishop, who had Protestant sympathies anyhow, and who ordered the vicar to recant openly in the pulpit next Sunday. Simons departed 'with a flea in his ear' and religion in the parish church, as elsewhere in England, began its troubled half-century of change via Henry VIII's 'Anglo-Catholicism' to Edward VI's Protestantism, Mary's Roman Catholicism, and then to Elizabeth's Establishment, in many of its features representing a middle way, claiming to protest against papal authority but to accept the traditional ministry and creeds.

At Windsor, a key man in the Reformation struggles was the organist at St George's, John Marbeck.[8] Appointed in 1531, he soon became a convinced reformer, and together with two lay clerks (perhaps those who sang the 'Nons'), Testwood and Benett, in 1544 was indicted before Bishop Capon, who heard their case accompanied by the then Dean and other commissioners. The trial adjourned, and ended at Windsor on 26 July, with a jury formed, it seems, of tenants of the Dean and Canons. The three were found guilty and were condemned to the stake. Marbeck, however, was reprieved after Bishop Gardiner of Winchester had interceded for him, perhaps recognising in him the great musician he was. Testwood, Benett, and the Filmer already encountered, suffered death at a spot near the present St George's Choir school, off Datchet Road. As they passed through the streets of Windsor they shouted to the townspeople to stand fast in the truth of the gospel. On being bound to the stake, one victim 'pulling the straw unto him, laid a good deal thereof upon the top of his head, saying 'This is God's hat, now am I dressed like a true soldier of Christ' '. In his published narrative Foxe printed (much later, in 1563) there is a woodcut of the grisly scene. The 'Windsor Martyrs' became heroes of the reformers.[9] Marbeck continued on his way. He compiled a great Biblical Concordance, and in 1549 set the first Book of Common Prayer to music. It is ironic to observe that the Anglo-Catholic movement of the 19th century found the reformer Marbeck's work a great help. His setting of the mass is now well-known throughout the Anglican communion and, incidentally, provided the music for the creed at Queen Elizabeth II's Coronation. The half-timbered building on the north wall of the Lower Ward opposite to the Nave of St George's is reputedly where Marbeck lived, and is known as 'Marbeck's'.

Dramatic as were these events, a potentially equally catastrophic development threatened Windsor five years after the burnings. Henry VIII died in 1547. His young son, Edward VI, reigned under the care of a 'Protector', Lord Somerset, whose arbitrary ways led to friction in the King's Council. Somerset played a trump card by taking the King from London to Windsor Castle under guard of 500 soldiers. He then began to fortify the Castle against his enemies – the first time this had happened for 3 centuries. His enemies retaliated by fortifying London and calling for a thousand men to march on Windsor. In fact, it all ended tamely. Only a captain of the guard went to Windsor, followed by the Lord Chancellor and the Council. Somerset neither fought nor imprisoned them. They entered the Castle, took charge by psychological rather than military tactics, and then had Somerset arrested. He was imprisoned here in Beauchamp's Tower; then removed to the Tower of London, and eventually, executed.[10] For Windsor at least, the day of great sieges had passed.

The Reformation mattered; but Lord Somerset did not. Windsor continued on its prosperous way. A key date had been passed in 1501 when the earliest known Windsor charity had been established, that of Thomas Hunte, on the edge of the built-up area, in Sheet Street.[11] In 1575 Franklyn's almshouses were built in Moor Street (now Park Street). Then at another of the town's ends, by Pucket's Close (at the bottom of Sheet Street) a pest house was constructed with a walled garden for sufferers from the plague. Plague had not ended in 1349; it was recurrent into the 1600s, but until 1575 those afflicted had had to live in hutches in the Worth field. The pest house by the 1700s was no longer needed, and was rebuilt in 1733 as a workhouse for the poor, where sail-cloth was laboriously made. Larger

A view from the North Terrace, Windsor Castle, by Paul Sandby. Reproduced by gracious permission of Her Majesty the Queen.

workhouses then appeared and the original pest house site in 1805 contained a gaol; a mid 19th century photograph shows it as a police station and is within the precincts of the infantry barracks. Windsor, however, with these examples, however elementary by our notions, as a community was starting to be self-conscious with some sense of duty towards the poor and the sick.

Moreover, the town was becoming more splendid. In 1585 an Act of Parliament was passed in order that Windsor's streets which had been 'yearly impaired and made noisome and foul by reason of the great and daily carriage and re-carriage' to Her Majesty's Castle, should be entirely paved – that is, with cobble-stones. The Market House, seen in Norden's map of 1607, was begun in 1586. This was just in time for one of the great royal receptions of the many Windsor has enjoyed. Elizabeth I though ceaselessly peripatetic like her mediaeval predecessors, did make use of Windsor and as it has been recently pointed out astonished her contemporaries because she 'not only installed a bath in Windsor Castle, but also took a bath herself once a month, whether she needed it or no'.[12]

Elizabeth's favour towards Windsor was shown by a State Entry on August 10th 1586, when she was received by the Mayor and Corporation in the then Guildhall (in Church Street). She was presented with the town's Mace and also with a petition on behalf of 'your poor townspeople inhabiting this ancient borough of Windsor.' Edward Hake, barrister and subsequently Mayor, made a speech that acquired fame from being printed the next year. He celebrated the Queen's Birthday, claiming God's protection since 'The power of man has been against us; the strength of the earth has attempted to invade us; Princes have conspired, nations have combined, subjects have become traitors, have rebelled, but God has protected.' And 'the inhabitants of this town of Windsor while others can only say and speak by report of the Queen, they can say and see her, to their unspeakable comfort.'[13]

A little later, a German visitor to Windsor, Paul Hentzner, saw it as an almost idyllic place. Returning from Eton College to his inn he 'happened to meet some country people celebrating harvest-home: their last load of corn they crown with flowers, having beside an image richly dressed, by which, perhaps, they would signify Ceres; this they keep moving about while men and women, men and maid-servants, riding through the streets in the cart, shout as loud as they can, till they arrive at the barn. The farmers here do not bind up their corn in sheaves, as they do with us; but directly as they have reaped or mowed it, put it into carts, and convey it into their barns.'[14]

Hentzner cannot, however, vie with Shakespeare in immortalising Windsor. It is *The Merry Wives of Windsor* which still represents to many the town of Windsor and its life under the Tudors. Tighe and Davis have shown how in this play Shakespeare reveals a close knowledge of Windsor, having walked its streets and fields and lived in at least one of its inns.[15] It is likely that *The Merry Wives* was written for a feast of the Order of the Garter held, not at Windsor, but at Whitehall Palace, in 1597.[16] In Act V the elves are told to make Windsor Castle worthy of the Queen, and to prepare the choir properly – and although the feast was at Whitehall in 1597, an Installation of new Knights did in fact take place in St George's choir a month later.

> 'The several chairs of order look you scour
> With juice of balm and every precious flower;
> Each fair instalment, coat and sev'ral crest,
> With loyal blazon, evermore be blest;
> And nightly, meadow fairies, look you sing,
> Like to the Garter's compass, in a ring:'

But it is the townspeople of Windsor, together with Sir John Falstaff, who dominate the play. And some at least of them may have been taken from life. Mine Host of the Garter Inn was probably Richard Gallys, a wealthy burgess, Mayor of Windsor, who also from 1563 to 1567 had served as one of Windsor's two representatives in Parliament, returning there in 1572 until his death in about 1583. He certainly would have considered himself the equal of Sir John and not hesitated to call him, as Shakespeare puts it, 'my bully-rook'. The two leading citizens may also have been local portraits

A view through Windsor Town Gate, by Paul Sandby. Reproduced by gracious permission of Her Majesty the Queen.

– Tighe and Davis observe that a Master Ford had a house nearly opposite the Garter Inn under the walls of the Castle, in Thames Street, and the name of Ford appears in the Parish Register of baptisms in 1598. The name of Page turns up in 1623 when fees were paid for the burials of Richard Page and of Anne Ford. But to Windsor history the play is perhaps of most interest for the way it depicts the still-mediaeval scene. Windsor still encircled the castle. Mine Host tells Doctor Caius to 'go about the fields with me through Frogmore', that is, down Thames Street and round the north of the castle to Frogmore fields. Page, Shallow, and Slender then went the other way round, along High Street and Park Street, to Frogmore. The Castle ditch, Herne's Oak, the Windsor bell striking twelve, and Datchet Mead help to fix the play firmly in a well-remembered town – notably Datchet meadow, the scene of Falstaff's final discomfiture, when he is carried in a basket of clothes from Ford's house to Datchet Mead, to be 'thrown into the Thames like a barrow of butcher's offal'.

Shakespeare's play is, in a sense, the last Windsor event of the Tudor era. Queen Elizabeth died in 1603, to be succeeded by a king, James I, whose reign ushered in for the whole country a period of further strife, which, to some extent, was a replay of the Reformation disputes of a century before.

Windsor Castle from Sheet Street, by Paul Sandby. Reproduced by gracious permission of Her Majesty the Queen.

James and his son Charles I tended to favour the Catholic half of the tentative Catholic-Protestant balance of Elizabeth. A Protestant or Puritan backlash was soon apparent in Windsor. One of the canons appointed by James I in 1617, Dr Godfrey Goodman, was about as advanced an 'Anglo-Catholic' (in modern terms) as James could have found.[17] Goodman steadily advanced in royal favour and was given the Bishopric of Gloucester in 1625. Goodman took a great interest in borough life. In this he was aided by the appointment of a Berkshire, that is Reading, man, William Laud, as Archbishop of Canterbury in 1633, another high churchman, and especially by the institution of yet another high churchman, John Cleaver, as Vicar of Windsor in the same year. Laudian developments appeared in Windsor.[18] In 1633 – 4 a new vestry was built for the church; the chancel was paved and wainscotted; the altar once more set at the east end of the chancel, and communion rails constructed. In 1635 a saints' bell was installed; surplices, flagons and chalices (one given by Archbishop Laud) were acquired. What was, on the whole, a Puritan Windsor tolerated these 'popish' developments until in the third year of change, 1635, it all became too much. Goodman 'at his proper cost' had ordered the 14th century market cross near the Market House to be repaired and decorated with painted carvings of the Crucifixion and Resurrection. The Mayor 'in the name of the whole town' begged Goodman not to add these religious emblems. Goodman the next day sent a letter back to the Mayor saying that if the king disliked the Crucifix (most unlikely), it would 'in an instant be blotted out'. Goodman reminded the Mayor that Windsor had a bad name for Puritanism – but he had hoped 'that all such fancies and humours had been buried with Mr Martin [the previous Vicar], for sure I am that your now Minister [Cleaver] broacheth no such doctrine'. Goodman said that he wrote 'with a little passion'. The Mayor complained to King Charles; the king did nothing. Goodman's crucifix stayed until the beginning of the Civil War, when it was quickly destroyed.

This municipal storm in a tea-cup was being repeated a hundred times elsewhere in the country, and was made infinitely more serious by political and social stresses, eventually focused in a straight conflict between Charles and Parliament. On 22 August 1642 Charles raised his standard at Nottingham against Parliament. The Civil War had started.

Raymond South in his *Royal Castle, Rebel Town* (1981) has so effectively described what the Civil War meant for Windsor that detailed repetition is unnecessary. But what were certainly some of the most important events in Windsor's life since the siege of 1216 cannot be passed over completely.[19]

Charles's first instinct, even before he raised his standard at Nottingham in 1642, had been to make Windsor his headquarters. In January he had been in the Castle and was reported to be raising troops there. Windsor, however, was too near the hostile capital, and the town itself was obviously far from Royalist. Within a month, therefore, Charles left Windsor for York, and as Mr South observes, the Castle was there for Parliament's taking. On 28 October forces loyal to Parliament occupied Windsor and they stayed there, in control, throughout the war. An immediate attempt was made, however, to dislodge them by Prince Rupert. He brought forces to Eton and with 'five pieces of Ordnance' bombarded town and castle for seven hours. A pamphleteer in *Joyful Tidings from Windsor* wrote that the town had been 'mightily battered and ruined, and the inhabitants very much damnified'. Little impression in fact was made on the Castle. The attack was a fiasco.

Subsequently, between 1642 and 1648, Windsor became a principal Puritan garrison town, a prison for Royalist soldiers, and, also, the training ground for a new type of army. The good Puritans of Windsor must have suffered, however willingly, more from this than from Rupert's bombardment. At one moment, in April 1643, some 16,000 foot and 3,000 horse under the Earl of Essex set out from Windsor, and, a little later, some 4000 soldiers were quartered at Windsor. Its permanent garrison was perhaps about a thousand, nearly as many as the town's total population.

Since the Castle provided no 'barracks' (a later invention) the townspeople had those soldiers who were not temporarily bivouacking in the Park billeted in their own homes – from where presumably at dawn hundreds of men would emerge for drill in the park or guard duty in the Castle. Householders (there were about 300 houses in the town) had to provide food and lodging; they were paid by the soldiers, but as the soldiers themselves often had their pay in considerable arrears, the billeting could not have been very profitable. Soldiers in 1643 committed irritating depredations in the Park, and by 1648 had killed and eaten practically all the several thousand deer there.

The most significant event for Windsor was neither the bombardment nor the billeting, but the formation, largely within the single month of April 1645, by Sir Thomas Fairfax, Captain-General of the New Model Army, of a trained company of professional soldiers at the initiative of Oliver Cromwell. Solders came to Fairfax in numbers; he inspired by Montgomery-like harangues and by his religious fervour. Sergeants and corporals were ready to accept demotion in order to serve Fairfax as common soldiers. The House of Commons sent quantities of weapons to Windsor. 1000 saddles, bridles and 'furniture', 1000 pairs of holsters and pistols and 500 pairs of spare holsters came, for instance on 29 April 1645. The next day, the New Model Army left Windsor, and the very threat of its advance caused the royalists to abandon Taunton, the first objective of the Puritan army.

Windsor remained as a military centre to which disbanded soldiers tended to return for payment or more work. Money and victuals ran out. Near the end of the fighting, in July 1648, the Castle was 'full of want and full of danger', but by November it had again become the Army headquarters. To it King Charles was brought after his capture, accompanied by his two dogs, a greyhound and a spaniel. Some Windsor people welcomed him, and Charles was happy to be back in his favourite town. But on 19 January 1649 Charles was taken from Windsor to London. His trial began in Westminster Hall on 20 January 1649 and on 30 January he was executed in Whitehall.

Windsor Castle was chosen as his place of burial[20] – probably for the same reason that led Richard III to have Henry VI interred there in 1471. Popular demonstrations could be kept well under control. The coffin was brought to the Deanery and placed on a table in the Hall. The table may have been the sturdy 17th century oak table which now has an honoured place in the Dean's Library on the first floor, though it probably began life in his kitchen or hall. After the king's coffin had been removed to the Royal Apartments in the Upper Ward, the next day, the 9th February, a sombre procession moved down to St George's in a snow storm. Without prayers, the coffin was laid in an accidentally discovered, but unmarked, vault in the centre of the choir. This was found to hold the coffins of Henry VIII and Queen Jane Seymour. A new Puritan Vicar of Windsor (the high-church Cleaver had died in 1648) entered in his Parish Register of burials, '[February] 9. King Charles in the Castle'. The royal free chapel of St George had been dispersed; its records and registers seized; the incumbent of the parish was very fairly the appropriate chronicler of the burial.

Windsor, both town and castle, by 1649 had very decisively taken sides, as, for that matter, had most of the country, between monarchy and republic. But ten years of the Commonwealth with its ebb and flow of military and religious dictatorship, followed by the death of Oliver Cromwell in 1658 and the almost total fatuity of his heir, Richard, brought about the restoration of the Monarchy in 1660. Windsor, although for nearly two centuries retaining a certain Puritan or Whiggish reserve so far as the monarchy was concerned, once more became a focus of royal government, and after 1660 received the sort of stimulus social, economic and architectural, it had received from the first Tudor monarchs. If Henry VIII's reign had had a flavour of a golden age about it for Windsor, so it was to prove had that of Charles II.

Notably, although we can not see very much of them today, new examples of fresh styles in art and architecture flooded into Windsor. Charles II and, for that matter, his brother, James II, were baroque in artistic taste as well as in personal behaviour. The long-established gothic tradition was finally thrust aside, and the age was that of Sir Christopher Wren, probably the greatest architect this country has known. Wren was himself a Windsor man, son of the Dean Christopher Wren who had faced the Puritan governor of the Castle in 1643, refusing to give up the keys to him and hiding some of the chapel treasure. The son (then only aged three) grew up eventually to be appointed Surveyor-General of Charles II's royal works, and the builder not only of St Paul's Cathedral, but of some 52 other city churches which had been destroyed in the fire of London. At Windsor, Charles II's most audacious use of Wren's genius came to nothing. The King resolved that his father, buried under unmarked stones

The Castle from Isherwood's Brew House, Datchet Lane, by Paul Sandby. Reproduced by gracious permission of Her Majesty the Queen.

in St George's Chapel, should have a magnificent mausoleum for his reburial. The first St George's (the building of 1240 which is now the Albert Memorial Chapel) was to be demolished, and in its place would arise what can only be described as a miniature St Paul's Cathedral. The original drawings by Wren for it survive in All Souls' College, Oxford, and, together with specifications of 1678 indicate a lofty circular building surmounted by a dome. Gilt-brass figures 'of the Great Life' were to be placed on every half-column. The diameter of the mausoleum was to be 72 feet, and its height, 150 feet. Either a marble or a gilt-bronze monument to Charles I (of a most dramatic character with writhing bodies of the dead) was to be placed within the building.[21]

The mausoleum was never built. The King's death seven years later, in 1685, effectively stopped tentative preliminary work. Incongruous as the Wren plans may now seem, they were undoubtedly in keeping with contemporary taste, and would have fitted in well with the other building works of the time being carried out in the Upper Ward, not by Wren but by Hugh May. A large section of the royal apartments was rebuilt. Outwardly it became, as Sir Owen Morshead comments, 'a mere box',[22] but inwardly it was full of 'voluptuous splendours'. Two are still there today: Charles II's private dining room with its profusion of game, fish, and fruit carved in limewood by Grinling Gibbons; and three splendid painted ceilings by Antonio Verrio, who began working at Windsor in 1675. But the *chef-d'oeuvre*, a superb royal chapel, elaborately decorated, the greatest work of the Italianizing movement at Windsor,[23] was ruthlessly destroyed by Wyatville a century or so later. Throughout much of the Castle, gothic pointed windows were destroyed, being replaced by semi-circular un-mullioned windows. Just six of these survive today – in the Henry III Tower. East and South terraces were constructed to continue the North Terrace, and a grand avenue, 3 miles long, was formed, cutting across the Sheet common field of the borough. This avenue survives today as the Long Walk, and it is a reminder that Charles II's Windsor was aiming at the great vistas as well as the baroque splendours of Louis XIV's contemporary palace at Versailles.

Charles II had a strong affection for Windsor.[24] In the later years of his reign, when July came, he retired to Windsor for hunting, racing, fishing, hawking, and a general life of pleasure (which did, however, include frequent appearances at service in St George's Chapel). His presence at Windsor with a large household led to a good deal of overcrowding. In 1674 the Dean was informed that 'His Majesty, intending with his whole Court to be at Windsor Castle the greater part of this summer' would need help to lodge the Knights of the Garter, the nobility and others of the Court. The Duke of York in fact took up permanent residence in the Deanery, and lowlier members of the Court must have squashed uncomfortably into the Lay Clerks' lodgings rather as Louis XIV's courtiers were being at the same time packed into the attics at Versailles. Charles II's mistress, however, Nell Gwynn, had a house especially built for her (Burford House), just outside the Castle walls, and her descendants, the Beauclerks, Dukes of St Albans, came to play a considerable part in the life of the borough – as the present 'St Alban's Street' commemorates. The town, in fact, benefited from Charles II's presence in many ways. Not only did they see daily cavalcades of sportsmen – all incidentally needing some of the trading services provided by the town – but they might also be treated to more magnificent spectacles. Evelyn describes in his diary for August 1674 how in one of the Little Park meadows in Underore 'a representation of the City of Maestricht, newly taken by the French' had been built. The siege was then re-enacted, 'Being night, it made a formidable show'.[25]

There was much coming and going. From 1673 a daily coach service was provided to London, and from 1674 a daily post (though only when the Court was in residence).[26] Houses were extensively rebuilt or refaced. We pass from the mediaeval half-timbered structures to the age of brick, and Windsor's new classical-type brick town houses were exceptionally large. No fewer than 22 out of 271 houses in 1663 had ten or more hearths; many more had from 6 to 9. The average number of hearths in a house in Windsor was 4.6, compared with 2.4 in Leicester and 2.6 in Exeter. Many of these, were, of course, inns.[27] Hartshorne's inn, for instance, in Peascod Street, had eleven hearths. But others must have been built, not only to house the courtiers overflowing from the Castle, but also to take the new permanent garrison. For the first time Windsor had become a garrison town. The New Model Army had gone, but a large military presence continued. 300 soldiers were quartered in inns and houses in 1660, although, ten years later, one of the three companies was absorbed into the Castle.[27] Soldiers became, as they remain today, an important if shifting element in the life of the borough.

Population was growing. About 1,700 in 1676; 2,000 in 1742; 4,049 in 1801.[28] But, as 18th century writers noted, there was a want of manufacture (as distinct from service industries). Brewing and malting alone were on any scale. Small-scale trades were confined to clock-making by the Davis family; the making of sail-cloth in the workhouse; and the tanning of leather by the Thames. As late as 1830 there was no manufacturing class; the Town council oligarchs were suppliers of food, drink, and provisions. Above all, farming had ceased to matter. The common fields as complete entities had gone, and the increasing acquisition of land by the Crown hastened the process. William III added to the royal estates Mill Common and other common fields between the Castle and the river. This, in conjunction with Charles II's elimination of much of the Sheet field, made the provision of services rather than farming Windsor's main function.

For Windsor borough the symbol of the baroque age was its new Guildhall. This has survived, whereas nearly all the baroque works in the Castle have gone. The Guildhall was designed in about 1687[29] by Sir Thomas Fitch, Surveyor of the Cinque Ports and a member of the London Carpenters' Company – he had delighted the City Corporation by the skill with which he had cut and wharfed the noisome Fleet Ditch in 1674. A knighthood followed and the quite prestigious commission for a 'Court House' in Windsor. Fitch died, however, in 1689, and the building was completed by Wren. Pevsner records, cautiously, the story that the Tuscan columns on the open ground floor do not actually reach the ceiling above 'as the sign of Wren's secret insistence on knowing more about the security of structure than the council who insisted on columns.'[30] Wren left the adjoining half-timbered structures on the east. These were swept away in 1829 and James Thomas Bedborough, a Windsor builder of whom much will be heard later, erected the present red-brick annex as a useful and

The entry in the Parish Register of the burial of Charles I, in Windsor Parish Church.

A Horse Race near Datchet Ferry on August 24th 1684.

acceptable extension of the Fitch-Wren building. Queen Anne's statue looks out northwards; her husband, Prince George of Denmark, southwards. Underneath Anne's statue, in latin, is carved the Mayor's advice to the sculptor, 'By your art, O Sculptor, Anne cannot be imitated; if you wish to represent Anne, carve a Goddess.'; a typically baroque flourish at the end of the Stuart epoch.

References

1 W.G. Hoskins, *Local History in England* (1959), 177.
2 op. cit., 176.
3 TD, i, 476.
4 ibid., 475 – 7.
5 ibid., 594 – 6.
6 ibid., 533.
7 The relevant section of John Foxe's *Acts and Munuments* (1563), known as *The Book of Martyrs* is conveniently reproduced in TD, i, 527 – 551.
8 E.H. Fellowes, 'Organists and Masters of the Choristers of St George's Chapel in Windsor Castle' (HM St G) (1939), 11 – 21.
9 See note 7 above.
10 TD, i, 582 – 6.
11 TD, ii, 632 – 40 for a valuable summary of Windsor charities based on the report of the Commission of Inquiry concerning Charities, 1818 – 1837 printed in Parliamentary Papers.

12 A. Laing, *Country Life* 27 May 1982, 10 – 12.
13 John Nichols, *The Progresses and Public Processions of Queen Elizabeth* (1823) 460 – 480.
14 Paul Hentzner's *Travels in England during the reign of Queen Elizabeth* were first translated by Horace Walpole (1797), see pp 55 – 6.
15 TD, i, chapter 24.
16 *The Merry Wives of Windsor* ed. H.J. Oliver (1971), xlv – xlvii, referring to the arguments of Leslie Hotson.
17 G.I. Soden, *Godfrey Goodman, Bishop of Gloucester, 1583 – 1656* (1953), and Goodman's own valuable *Court of St James I* (ed. J.S. Brewer, 1839).
18 Harwood, 344 – 6; TD, ii, 98 – 111.
19 For references concerning the period of the Civil War see R. South, op.cit., 103 – 5. See also Mr South's 'St George's under the Puritans' RF St G (1980 – 1), 56 – 64.
20 Maurice Bond 'Burial Places of the English Monarchs' RF St G (1969 – 70), 36 – 8.
21 Hope, 485.
22 Owen Morshead, *Windsor Castle* 2nd. ed. (1957), 64.
23 Hope, 323.
24 See TD, ii, 365 – 407. The St George's Chapel Act Book, VI.B. 14, records that the King came to Chapel on Sundays and holidays and people crowded on to the leads by the (then plain-glass) East Window to gaze at him in his pew, the Edward IV chantry. The canons resolved that 'it is undecent anybody should gaze upon his Majeste' and various doors were to be nailed or even bricked up. (p.201).
25 TD, ii, 365.
26 S. Bond, *The First Hall Book* (1968), xi.
27 See R. South op.cit., 96; and on quartering in general, C. Walton *History of the British Standing Army* (1894), 714 – 719.
28 J. Langton, *The Second Hall Book* (1973), vii.
29 Thesis by Ayrton Grime, 'Windsor Guildhall' in BRO.
30 Pevsner, *Berkshire*, 301.

Georgian Windsor

What did visitors make of the Windsor inherited by the Hanoverians from the Stuarts? We have two highly articulate tourists through whose eyes it can be seen: Celia Fiennes came to it in 1698 and again in about 1703, and Daniel Defoe, of *Robinson Crusoe* fame, in a *Tour Through England and Wales*, published between 1724 and 1728, gave an elaborate account of Windsor. Celia, a Whiggish nonconformist member of Viscount Saye and Sele's family (with 'an eye like a gimlet') approached Windsor from Bagshot across the forest and park. 'This way most clay deep way, the worse by reason of the rains and full of sloughs'. The Castle then appeared, 'standing on a hill much after the manner of Durham', and it was 'a pretty great ascent to the town' (by Peascod Street?)[1]. She liked the town, it was 'well-built something suitable to London by reason of its affinity to the Court'. The streets were large, and she was impressed by 'the Market Cross on stone pillars and a large Hall on the top' (the Guildhall). The Castle was to her two separate places, the 'Cathedral' (St George's Chapel) and 'the Castle'. St George's was 'very fine built all stone and carved on the outside; several Cloisters lead to the Doctors' (Canons') houses, it's a lofty noble building.' She admired the very high, curiously carved roof, a 'very large fine organ', an altar 'crimson velvet striped with gold tissue large candlesticks and basons gilt'. She showed what is also nowadays current enthusiasm for the Rutland chantry with its 'very fine monument' (of the de Roos's) and also the Lincoln chapel, with the roll of matt under the head of the Lord and Lady 'that was so natural looked like real matt'. Puritan or no, she found her Cathedral a great experience.

From it she 'proceeded on to the Castle which is the finest palace the king has, especially now Whitehall is burnt' (in 1698). In the Apartments she admired 'a great prospect of the whole town and Windsor Forest, the country round to Kensington' with the Thames 'which twists and turns it self round the meadows and grounds'. Noble halls, the Chamber of State 'very lofty and painted on the roof', and a State Drawing Room, very glorious and newly made 'to give audience to the French Ambassador to show the grandeur and magnificence of the British Monarch' completed her tour. She finishes by saying that 'some of these fooleries are requisite sometimes to create admiration and regard to keep up the state of a king and nation'. Her Puritanism had been overcome by the Cathedral, but as a Whig she had reserves about the Castle.

With Defoe we have a similar sort of outlook, very conscious not of tradition, but of new commerce and industry. Yet when he comes to

A painting by Canaletto in 1747, during a visit to England.

Windsor he is simply overwhelmed.[2] 'I must take leave talking of trade, navigation, meal, and malt, and describe the most beautiful and most pleasantly situated castle, and royal palace, in the whole isle of Britain.' The town he ignored, plunging, after some history, into his tour of the Castle. He starts with the terrace, built, he says, by Queen Elizabeth, where she loved to walk, with an umbrella if it rained. It is 'a magnificent work . . . a noble walk . . . neither at Versailles, or at any of the royal palaces in France, or at Rome, or at Naples, have I seen anything like it' (the nearest to it, he thought, was the Tokapi Palace at Constantinople, true enough, even today). The apartments he admired, notably the Chapel Royal of Charles II. Unlike Celia, he thought the Lower Ward 'not so beautiful', though the Chapel 'is not only fine within, but the workmanship without is extraordinary; nothing so ancient is to be seen so very beautiful'. This often bitterly critical man had been captivated by Windsor. Beauty, tradition and architecture were not antipathetic to industrial development in the early eighteenth century.

Queen Anne had loved living in the castle, racing at Ascot, and stag-hunting in the Park. Her successors, George I (1714 – 1727) and George II (1727 – 1760) seldom came to Windsor and did little for the maintenance of the Castle. Owen Morshead summarised their attitude as a dislike of the place combined with a refusal to spend money – of which, as it turned out, much was needed – on the maintenance and repair of Charles II's splendid and lavish building.[3] The first two Hanoverian monarchs felt more at home in Kensington Palace and Hampton Court.[4] 'Queen Anne is dead' therefore had a very real significance for both castle and borough. Now occurred what Owen Morshead calls 'the Dark Ages'. Private individuals were let lodgings in the Upper Ward; the present Garter Room became an Office of Works headquarters. The Dean and Canons lost interest in Windsor and left the daily services to be sung (still with an impressive repertoire) by the Minor Canons and Lay Clerks. Windsor was only nominally royal.

Yet Windsor's development did not entirely cease. It had been given considerable impetus by Charles II, his courtiers, and the descendants of Nell Gwynn. Prominent families came to live in Windsor to an extent unknown previously, and not to recur until the end of the 19th century. The Beauclerks not only lived in what is now St Albans Street, they accepted municipal office, joining on the council the innkeepers, barbers and bricklayers who formed the main oligarchy. Lord George Beauclerk, M.P., aide-de-camp to George II and Lord Sidney, the Vice-Chamberlain of the Royal Household were very much Windsor personalities. Other Windsor councillors included Lord Vere of Hanworth, M.P., the Lord Lieutenant of Berkshire and the Earl of Cholmondeley, M.P., Lord Privy Seal in 1743. Pote's guidebook of 1755, *Les Delices de Windsore* describes 'the Houses of the Nobility and Gentry that reside in the adjacent Neighbourhood', forming a principal part of the 'delightful prospect' of Windsor – Lord

Harry Beauclerk in a house at Winkfield, the Duke of Roxburgh and the Hon. James Bateman (in 'a most agreeable villa') at Old Windsor, the Earl of Cardigan at Ditton Park, the Duke of Marlborough at Langley Park, and so on. But after touring the houses of the nobility Pote brings us back to Windsor itself, where, he reminds us 'every good Accommodation is equally to be found'.

Some of this 'good accommodation' happily survives. Best of all is a group of houses in the entirely excellent Park Street, where nos. 4 to 6 are unaltered from the 1700s (apart from no. 5's bay window). No. 4, now a solicitors' office (where for long Town Clerks had custody of the Borough charters) has a great deal of attractive detail, with roundel masks, fluted pilasters and a six panelled door, and includes an entrance to Black Lion Yard beyond. The most splendid house of this type came at the end of the century, Hadleigh House, set back from Sheet Street behind a walled courtyard, and although with five storeys (including attic and basement) only one room thick, with a fine view of the Long Walk on the south side. But the most important of all Windsor's great town houses has gone: Pilgrim Place, at the corner of Peascod Street and William Street.[5] Here lived Richard Topham, the nation's archivist, who was not only Keeper of the Records at the Tower of London, but also M.P. for Windsor from 1698 to 1713, and Lord of the Manor for Clewer Brocas. His house was a collector's paradise. Pope says in his fourth *Moral Essay* that rich connoisseurs bought 'For Topham drawings and designs'. The collections were bequeathed to Eton College. His remaining property passed to his sister Arabella, and then, on her death in 1732, to her husband, Sir Thomas Reeve, Lord Chief Justice of the Common Pleas. This great man she must have met in Peascod Street, for his father, Richard Reeve, was a neighbour, innkeeper of the Maidenhead there. Pilgrim Place then passed via Lord Sidney to his son Topham Beauclerk. Topham was a councillor; more interestingly, he was a friend of Dr. Samuel Johnson, who came to stay at Pilgrim Place 'where he was entertained with experiments in natural philosophy'.

Windsor with so many noblemen and gentry settled in and around it might be though necessarily to have become part of the 'establishment', in the modern phrase. Not so. A long-running dispute between the inhabitants and the fraternity (or council) had ended in the victory of the inhabitants in 1690, whereby the two members returned by the borough to sit in the House of Commons should be elected by all those paying 'scot and lot', roughly what we might call ratepayers or householders. Of these there were between 300 and 400 in the eighteenth century. At the elections, held at the Guildhall, each had the duty to stand up and declare his vote.[6] During the century there were some 38 elections, and Windsor proved to be by no means a 'pocket' or 'Court' borough (unlike so many others before the

1832 Reform Act). John Brooke has recently commented that 'There was a large proportion of independent voters [at Windsor], and the borough was not easily managed'. The Duke of Cumberland for a time took some interest in it all from his home at Cumberland Lodge in the Great Park, as did equally his enemy, the Duke of St Albans, from Burford Lodge. Contests were 'expensive'. In 1757 a Jacobite or Tory group raised £5,000 to defeat the Whig candidate. Ten years later, a candidate was 'firmly determined to risk purse and everything else' to become Windsor's M.P. At first the borough had some respect for royal wishes. George II said that Windsor was his own borough, and in fact, until mid-century, court candidates were returned. Then opinions shifted. Admiral Augustus Keppel, whose family were notable local residents, was elected in 1768. He was strongly in opposition to the King and regarded himself as the 'town's man'; his colleague as M.P., Lord George Beauclerk, *per contra*, was the government's man. In 1780, however, both Windsor Members belonged to the opposition, and Keppel had by then made himself particularly obnoxious to George III. The King went so far as to say that Windsor's 'Corporation has ever been adverse to the Government' and in 1780 he paid out £2,600 from his private account in order to correct this lack of loyalty. The King canvassed Windsor tradesmen on behalf of his own candidate, Peniston Portlock Powney, a local landowner, and Powney just won by 16 votes. By 1806 a tacit arrangement, as Raymond South points out, had been achieved. One candidate would be recommended to the voters of Windsor by 'the countenance on the hill', the other by leading townspeople. This all ended in 1845, when Queen Victoria declared that she 'does not wish to interfere in Elections'.

During the period of the absence of the Court from Windsor some improvements, but only a few, in the life of the town had taken place. As we shall see later, in 1725 Windsor gained, belatedly, its first school of any real pretensions – it had never had the sort of 'grammar school' that could be found in so many market towns. In 1769 the main streets were paved, given lighting, and provided with six watchmen, but inertia seemed to be settling in. Jonathan Swift was not the only visitor to consider the town 'scoundrel', and even its garrison began to be removed. There were only 47 officers and men in 1730; the Castle's cannons were 'unserviceable'; the Round Tower, 'ruinous'. The gentry were surrounded by not very wealthy or vigorous tradespeople; and this at a time when, as Braudel comments 'everything improved' in the main European countries.

Improvement for Windsor came belatedly. Perhaps it might be considered to have been the result of the 17 year old Princess Charlotte of Mecklenburg-Strelitz marrying King George III in 1761. From the moment she saw Windsor she expressed a desire to reside there. Her life has been recently told in fascinating detail by Olwen Hedley,[7] herself a Windsorian

Drawing of Thames Street circa 1810 by John Claude Natles, showing the Curfew Tower with its original top.

and local historian. But she makes it clear that neither Queen Charlotte nor King George III seemed to have thought originally of using the Castle itself as a residence. Even 15 years later, in 1776, the King merely gave Charlotte a 'small neat house on Castle Hill' once used by Queen Anne. Then the family grew. As Miss Hedley says, 'with their train of nurses, rockers, laundresses, semptresses, necessary women, governesses and tutors' – and there were 15 children – the small Castle Hill house proved inadequate. It was therefore converted into a large mansion; the Duke of St Albans yielded up Burford House in 1777; and then finally, a section of the Upper Ward was brought once more into royal use, the south and east fronts. By 1778 Queen Charlotte was surrounded by her whole family in 'this sweet retreat.'

The Court had returned to Windsor, and until his death in 1820 George III remained closely associated with both the Castle and the town, bringing back the vitality of Charles II's days and setting in train architectural changes that produced, under his son, George IV, the Castle we know today. George III's essays in building were fairly tentative – a cloister in the State Apartments, now enclosed at first floor level to form the Waterloo Chamber, and a new State Entrance.[8] His son, George IV, who reigned from 1820 to 1830, was vastly more ambitious. The first architect had been the gifted James Wyatt, R.A., and 11 years after his death in 1813, his still more original and industrious nephew and apprentice, Jeffry Wyatt took charge. Jeffry occupied the Winchester Tower and remained there from 1824 to his death in 1840.[9] He began by changing his name to Wyatville, provoking the often quoted verse:

> 'Let George, whose restlessness leaves nothing quiet,
> Change if he must the good old name of Wyatt;
> But let us hope that their united skill
> Will not make Windsor Castle Wyatt Ville.'

But before Wyatville's works got under way a much humbler man had, at George III's command, achieved a more remarkable if more limited decorative and architectural revolution in the Lower Ward. This was Henry Emlyn. He worked for the Board of Works at the Castle, and was also carpenter to the Dean and Canons.[10] There was in the later 18th century a feeling that the Chapel was in at least as sorry a state as the rest of the Castle had been. *The Gentleman's Magazine* described it as 'perhaps the first in the world for beauty and splendour, but dirty and disregarded to such a degree as to become a nuisance to the eye and a reproach to the sextons'. This was printed in 1786.[11] But by then something had begun to happen. King George and Queen Charlotte were often in the Castle, and clearly preferred Sunday service in St George's to that in the Upper Ward chapel of Charles II. For the King, as for Celia Fiennes St George's was 'the cathedral' and for its repair he was ready, as it turned out, to spend some £16,000 of his own money. Emlyn between 1782 and 1785 had refurbished the Edward IV upper chantry which looks down on the High Altar. This again became a royal pew as it had been for Katharine of Aragon and also for Charles II. Emlyn repanelled the chantry adding the curved canopy, intricately and elegantly carved, as well as desks, chairs and other furniture. From here George III attended service, subsequently greeting the congregation in the vestry below. From here Queen Victoria watched the marriage of the Prince of Wales to Princess Alexandra; and here today is one of the side-chapels of St George's, used by the conference centre of St George's House, and also, as the white lamp seen from the choir aisle below witnesses, the place of reservation of the Blessed Sacrament.

By 1792 many other works had been completed in St George's: painted windows designed by Sir Benjamin West, together with a new carved reredos behind the high altar, the stunning canopy or tester over the Sovereign's stall, four more stalls for additional Knights of the Garter, and extensive additions and re-carving for the old stalls – the various gangways' doors now helpfully excluding draughts are all the work of

Emlyn. He gave a new organ its carved case; and, above all, he set up the present very grand organ loft made of Coade stone. Much else was done, with George III's backing; the document drawn up at the end was rightly entitled 'An Account of all the Great Works, 1782 – 1792'. Luckily Emlyn, by now famous, and in 1795 elected a Fellow of the Society of Antiquaries, did not go any further. He might have done. At heart he was not a mediaevalist but a classicist, and as early as 1786 he had planned to destroy the whole of the Chapel precincts, replacing them, as my wife has commented 'with a range of buildings in a classical style of extreme dullness.' The style was to be that of a new 'British Order' which was published by him in 1781, and in fact was then used when Henry Griffiths's country mansion was built in 1785 at Old Windsor (subsequently the Jesuits' Beaumont College). The columns there are double, to imitate the Forest oak trees; the capitals are decorated with garter plumes; and the star of the Garter appears between the volutes. Beaumont is unique; but it is as well that neither Wren nor Emlyn succeeded in so radically altering the Castle.

In fact, the Castle far from being made more classical in style, was altered back into something more mediaeval than even the Middle Ages had ever managed to produce. Sir Jeffry Wyatville destroyed nearly all Charles II's round-headed windows, as we have seen. A gothic gateway (St George's Gate) was erected at the Castle Hill entrance to the Castle; the neighbouring Brunswick and Devil's Towers, both highly mediaeval, are Wyatville's work, as is the extremely romantic and picturesque low defensive wall in the Middle Ward curving round to the north – arrow-slits, guard walk and all. The Round Tower was raised 33 feet and in keeping with this extra height, top floors were added to the main royal apartments. This created the castle outline we all know, and is certainly more dramatic on the sky-line than ever the dumpty towers of the mediaeval castle could have been. For the early 19th century, effect was vital, even if it produced some shams. Effect there certainly was, and also, sham. If one climbs to the top of the Round Tower there is only an empty hole inside until, looking down 33 feet, the roof of the mediaeval interior of the tower can be seen. Owen Morshead remarks that Wyatville was a good builder, but adds that he countenanced 'native deceits', and caustically notes that the dressed stones of Wyatville's new walls (which anyhow fitted perfectly) were supplied with unnecessary flints and mortar. 'The same effect could have been produced with adhesive tape'.[12] By the end of Wyatville's work he had created a much more commodious and useful royal palace, but the cost had reached the almost unbelievable figure of a million pounds in prices of that day.

The restoration of Windsor Castle on this vast scale can only be paralleled, though not surpassed, by Viollet-le-Duc's entire remaking of the

The Theatre Royal in High Street, in Georgian times.

fortifications of Avignon a generation later. The confidence of these great architects is breath-taking. They worked, however, with their age, when the spirit of the Romantic Movement produced for the first time 'the concept of a building as not only functional but also as a historic monument', justifying extraordinary architectural effort.[13] And, in the last resort, such buildings were felt, and are still felt, to have as well, an aesthetic quality independent of function or meaning. The visitor approaching Windsor from the south, on entering the Great Park by the Ascot Gate, sees in Wyatville's Castle, (for it is in the last resort, his,) a very splendid work of art.

This was all part of what for the town as well as for the Royal Family was a great blessing, the return of the Kings to their ancient home. Moreover, George III, unlike his predecessors, rode or walked about the streets and shopped. Trade looked up. Market stalls gave way to 'smart shops' as Olwen Hedley observes. The Queen's milliner, Mrs Caley, settled in Windsor and prospered, later, in 1823, moving to the fine new premises opposite the Guildhall where her successors still carry on millinery, as well as many other trades. The King and Queen went to Windsor Theatre, then in High Street, the King laughing so heartily that Charles Knight said, 'the walls shook'. Daily, the King rose at six, and then spent the morning visiting the royal dairy, and supervising the new Norfolk and Flemish farms (practising the new Flemish husbandries). 'George the Farmer' turned the Park from a hunting venue in part into a profitable agricultural exercise. Whatever the judgement on George as a king may be (and this is not now so harsh as it once was) as a landowner and a Windsor resident he is notable. George III would have had much in common with Prince Albert, who, in effect, a generation later, carried on from where George III had left off.

Some idea of Windsor life when George III and then his sons were on the throne is provided by a notebook, now in the Berkshire Record Office, which was kept by a Windsor cutler, George Pridie. Pridie had a shop at the lower end of Peascod Street, opposite what is now William Street and for long had been Pilgrim Place. Literate, even a versifier, Pridie's world, as Maitland Underhill has pointed out 'was his local parish, beyond his immediate Peascod Street associates he had contacts with the parson, doctor, lawyer and Parliamentary elections. Very distantly there was a King or Queen living up the hill in the Castle who was occasionally seen and who might let fall some word which was repeated in the Town.'[14] An example of this was in a September 1831 entry: 'Her Majesty Queen Adelaide had the housemaids before her at Windsor Castle and said I will have no silk gowns worn here and you must wear aprons'. The death of Princess Alice, seven years earlier had inspired Pridie to verse, opening:

'Booms from afar the minute gun;
And slowly tolls the solemn bell.
How swiftly heavy tidings run!
The Princess whom we loved so well
Is suddenly call'd home to God.'
And we must bow and kiss the rod'

(with four more verses). The Garrison was for Pridie a very important feature of town life and he noted in 1797 that 'The first Regiment that march'd into Windsor Infantry Barracks was the Coldstream Guards' in April; and, in 1804, 'The Horse Guards Blue first came to the Cavalry Barracks'. He calmly adds under a heading 'May 1830 Militry Torture', 'A Drummer Belonging to the first Regiment of Foot Guards was flogged on Tuesday Died on the Wednesday and Buried on Friday.'

The routine life of a small town clearly got much of its excitement from catastrophic events and these were separately categorised by Pridie. Thus, there were FIRES, with the Cavalry Barracks Mess House burnt down in 1808, Mr Knight's Stables in Sheet Street in 1822; ROBBERIES, when in 1830 Mr Egelstone's House, Brunswick Terrace, was broken open. Later Herbert Bass and Swain had sentence of death passed on them for house breaking at Datchet. Then a resident's garden was robbed of 170 pinks, and a Brewer's man of £12. For ACCIDENTS there were many entries. A workman in the Castle 'had both his legs taken off' (1827); a fishmonger's son fell from a tree in the Long Walk and broke his thigh (1829); a coachbuilder's servant was burned to death (1830). DEATHS, in particular added substance to Pridie's record, especially the bizarre entry for July 1831, that 'Old Haynes the Poor Knight Died. His effigy was Hung at the Market House at Williams Election for swearing and bribery.' Suicides occurred quite frequently. On 10 July 1836, 'Thomas Knowles, Hawker, was Bit with an Adder.'

The cultural life became important for Windsor's middle classes, as we shall see, during the nineteenth century, but Pridie was very much of the eighteenth. For him FIGHTS provided sufficient recreation. On Shrove Tuesday, 1830, there were six cockfights in Thumwood's Barn, Sheet Street; in March 'Samuel Bennett and Clark fought in the Rays at Clewer – Bennett won.' They fought again near Surly Hall in May, but two men were 'sent to jail for Insulting the Constable at the fight.' Later, one contestant 'died the same night', and a cockfight of 'Windsor and Eton against the Brighton Coachman' was 'brought to a Wrangle'. Pridie's other interest was the public house, and he paid great attention to the rebuilding of *The Bull* near him in Peascod Street in 1835, and of *The Ship* in Church Lane in 1828 (still a notable feature of the cobbled street area). Pridie clearly enjoyed his long Windsor life. He was diarising in 1787 and continued until 1858, by which time he must have been very near to 90 years old. He left a permanent memorial in the plaque which he, as cutler, engraved to be set on the wall of the Guildhall extension of 1829 – where it can still be seen.

Pridie gives us his highly personal and idiosyncratic view of Windsor in Georgian times. What is ultimately much more significant for the local historian is that in George III's reign local journalism effectively started. Joseph Pote had produced in 1745 a *Windsor and Eton Journal*, but it only lasted a few years, and so far as is known, the issue of 19 March 1747 owned by Mr Patrick Marlz is unique. However, on 1 August 1812 Charles Knight, bookseller, Alderman and (in 1806 and 1817–18), Mayor of Windsor produced the first number of the *Windsor and Eton Express.*[15] A Mr Richard Oxley became co-proprietor in 1833, and today, members of his family as 'Oxley and Son (Windsor) Ltd.' still direct the weekly publication of the *Express* from 4 High Street to which the firm moved in 1836.

From 1812 onwards the *Express* became a prime source of historical information for local historians, as well as for those other historians who wish to see how normal events were understood locally (and until this century much of the paper was devoted to national news). Between 1861 and 1900 there were in addition some eight competing papers. They did not

The Guildhall Chamber.

survive. The historian of Berkshire's press fairly notes that the *Express* (now the *Windsor, Slough and Eton Express*),[16] 'still exists as a flourishing, well-conducted weekly newspaper'. In this, Windsor borough today has as firm a link with the life of the Georgian town as in the many Georgian houses still surviving.

References

On the whole period further detail can be found in Angus Macnaghten's *Windsor and Eton in Georgian Times*.

1 ed. C. Morris, *The Journals of Celia Fiennes* (1959), 274 – 82, 357 – 61.
2 D. Defoe, *A Tour through England and Wales*, 2 Vols. (1928), i, 303 – 11.
3 O. Morshead, *Windsor Castle* (1957), 69.
4 Hope, 347.
5 Harwood, 148 – 153.
6 On the Parliamentary representation of Windsor, see *The First Hall Book* xxvii – xxviii, *The Second Hall Book*, xix – xx; *The Fifth Hall Book* (ed. R. South) xxvi – xxvii; Shelagh Bond *A List of Windsor Representatives in Parliament, 1302 – 1966*; BAJ (1965 – 6), 34 – 44; and the relevant volume of *The History of Parliament*.

7 Olwen Hedley, *Queen Charlotte* (1975).
8 Hope, 347 – 54.
9 Hope, 354 – 65, on which much of the remaining section of this chapter is based.
10 Shelagh Bond, 'Henry Emlyn of Windsor; a Craftsman of Skill and Invention' RF St G (1962), 99 – 103; Jane Roberts, 'Henry Emlyn's Restoration of St George's Chapel', RF St G (1976 – 7), 331 – 8. See also Dr. Loekman's 'Account of all the great work . . .', Hope 385 – 94.
11 *Gentleman's Magazine* (1786), part i, 449. See also Shelagh Bond, 'Monuments of St George's Chapel' (M St GC) (1958), xviii – xxvi.
12 Morshead, op.cit., contributes a masterly account of works under George IV in his chapter 8.
13 See Pierre de Lagarde, 'Le combat passionne' des e'cuvards francais pour leur patrimonie', *Historia*, no. 442, 84 – 92, for an interesting discussion of the new concept.
14 Pridie's MS diary is in BRO, together with Mr Underhill's transcript and manuscript introduction.
15 Charles senior was assisted by his son, another Charles (1791 – 1878), who became one of the most enterprising publishers of the century and a pioneer in the field of popular literature for the masses, notably through his production of the *Penny Cyclopedia* and a *Pictorial Shakespeare (Dictionary of National Biography*, sub. Knight, Charles).
16 K. G. Burton, *The Early Newspaper Press in Berkshire (1723 – 1855)*, (1954).

The Victorian Castle

The Windsor described by George Pridie (and chronicled in the *Express*) was Georgian, but Windsor as we know it today, where it is not mediaeval, seems to have an almost overwhelmingly Victorian flavour. The long reign of Queen Victoria, from 1837 to 1901, set its mark on the town and the Castle almost, as it seems, ineffaceably, partly in architecture, but also in manners and customs. Victoria married Prince Albert of Saxe-Coburg on 10 February, 1840, and their first Christmas was spent at Windsor, a Christmas tree being set up in the Castle, perhaps the beginning here of what is now universal custom.[1] And, in addition to inventing a new form of social ritual, Victoria and Albert popularised from Windsor the enjoyment of acting. Between 1848 and 1861 they had a steady sequence of theatrical performances especially enacted in the Castle, first in the Rubens Room, then, after 1845, in St George's Hall, with Charles Kean as Director of the Theatricals.[2] Towards the end of her reign, with a partial emergence from her long period of mourning, as we shall see, Victoria returned to this intensive royal patronage of both dramatic and operatic stars, again, almost entirely in a Windsor setting.

But the serious business of life for the Queen inevitably included in the early years a good deal of ceremonial, and, again, Windsor seemed the right setting for ceremonial. After her accession in 1837 she had held a review of Life Guards, Grenadier Guards and Lancers in the Park. 'She was mounted, wearing the Windsor uniform, dark blue with red collar and cuffs, the Order of the Garter and a military cap.' The Queen wrote later that 'The whole thing went off beautifully and I felt for the first time like a man, as if I could fight myself at the head of my Troops'.[3]

Windsor, Castle, Borough and Park, under Victoria, became the ideal centre for state visits, very much a Victorian invention. The Emperor Nicholas I of Russia in 1844 was given dinner in the Waterloo Chamber, reviewed the troops in the Park, and was 'quite enchanted by the Castle.[4] Later in the same year King Louis Philippe of France came to the Castle, exclaiming in the State Apartments, 'Dieu, comme c'est beau'.[5] Eleven years later, the most famous visit of all was when the Emperor Napoleon III and his Empress, Eugenie, were received by the Queen; the State bed in the apartments they occupied is still decorated with their initials NI EI.[6]

Yet Windsor, for Victoria and Albert, had its drawbacks. The Castle was badly managed and it still seemed, as it had once to Edward VI, rather like a prison. There were few gardens or walks with any privacy. Railways by the 1850s were bringing hundreds to the terraces where George III had probably only encountered dozens. The Home Park, although now royal and not burghal, was crossed by the main road to Staines, and in spite of the fence protecting it on both sides, the public stopped their carriages and climbed on to the roofs of them to watch for the royal couple and their family. This was, however, ingeniously remedied in 1848 when, in return for royal agreement to two railway stations in Windsor, the main highway was ended at Park Street and a more circuitous route, not crossing the Home Park, was constructed a mile to the south. So Frogmore House and its grounds became in 1849, as they have remained, an attractive private retreat for the royal family.[7]

A still worse problem for the Castle inhabitants was quite simply its drains. The town itself, as we shall see, had open ditches with effluent in them, and in 1848 the Lord Chamberlain reported on the 'noxious effluvia' in the old drains and cesspools of the Castle. Mrs Woodham Smith concludes that 'Beneath the splendour, Windsor Castle was more dangerous than a jungle.' It is even possible that the premature death of Prince Albert in 1861 from typhoid fever had been caused by the appalling drainage of the whole district.[8]

The Prince's death in 1861 at Windsor had two contrary effects on the Queen, partly binding her to Windsor, partly estranging her from it. The Prince's bedroom was kept exactly as it was at his death, and became a place of pilgrimage. His memorial was the spectacular reconstruction by the Queen of Wolsey's chapel in the Lower Ward as the Albert Memorial Chapel. The Prince was buried in a special mausoleum, in the traditions of his homeland, at Frogmore, within a dramatic new building, part Baroque, part Byzantine. Thereafter the St George's clergy were regularly performing memorial services at Frogmore in the Queen's presence. In a real sense Windsor acquired sanctity for her because of this, and the Castle was never abandoned, indeed much later coming back a good deal into the Queen's favour. But Osborne House in the Isle of Wight, completed in 1851, and Balmoral Castle in Aberdeenshire, completed in 1854, offered a deeply grieving widow much more privacy than could Windsor, and for the last 40 years of her reign, from 1861 to 1901, Windsor did not form a predominant part of the Queen's regime. Yet each year the Queen came to Windsor for some months. It was certainly more convenient for state business than Osborne or Balmoral. And Court Circulars quite late in her reign, from 1881 onwards, show that there was a good deal of variety and interest again at Windsor for her. Almost weekly, concert artists, or even whole operatic or dramatic casts, came to Windsor to perform in the State Apartments. The singer Paoli Tosti was *persona gratissima* with the Queen, and organised entertainment for her, though not always with the greatest of tact. Sir Frederic Ponsonby tells how equally famous, if rival singers, Jean and Edouard de Reszke, were not considered by Tosti good enough to have a meal at the Castle, and were sent to the *White Hart* in High Street. They

An oil painting of Windsor Castle by moonlight by the artist Henry Pether circa 1830.

consequently sang very 'apathetically'; the Queen asked why, objected, and thereafter the de Reszkes were treated at Windsor like Polish nobility.[9]

As Arthur Ponsonby commented, it was in due course natural 'that the inclination to enjoy a little fun and amusement should re-emerge if only to relieve the monotony of the routine which even she herself at times felt to be dull.'[10] And, of course, we are now realising that Victoria, far from being a philistine, was deeply interested in the arts. Drawing, music and acting were all very real and creative activities in her family. A telling reminder of this was provided by Marina Warner in 1979 when she published *Queen Victoria's Sketchbook* with some eloquent watercolour sketches of Windsor, Osborne and Balmoral. Moreover, members of her family entered into the life of Windsor with some enthusiasm. Prince Albert sponsored good working-class homes in Windsor, still known as the Prince Consort Cottages; as Gordon Cullingham has brilliantly described in a recent monograph, Prince Albert's youngest son, Prince Leopold, after his father's death, gave the strongest possible support to the establishment of the Royal Windsor Tapestry Manufactory of which Queen Victoria became Patron;[11] and Windsor still has a Princess Christian Nursing Home as one example of the unceasing interest the Queen's granddaughter, the second Princess Christian, took the most marked interest in local affairs.[12] Windsor's cultural societies benefited not only from royal patronage, but also, on occasion, from royal performances – Princess Christian was quite happy to sing solos in the Royal Albert Institute.

So, in a variety of ways, the royal connection re-established by George III became deeper and more influential under Victoria. It should be added that King George's love of St George's Chapel also was, though in a quite different way, reflected under Victoria. The Queen was in some sense bound to Windsor by the reliance she came to place successively on two remarkable Deans of St George's, Gerald Wellesley, nephew of the first Duke of Wellington (and looking exactly like him), who was Dean from 1854 to 1882,[13] and then Randall Davidson, the future Archbishop of Canterbury, Dean from 1883 to 1891.[14] Wellesley, as the Queen wrote 'knew all our children from their earliest years and three from their birth, shared every joy and sorrow as well as every trouble and anxiety'. In fact Dean Wellesley became, as Georgina Battiscombe has suggested, the *Eminence Grise*, without whose counsel no appointment, even to the premiership, was made. This happened to be particularly fortunate politically, for Wellesley was by way of being a Whig or even a Liberal, and he mediated helpfully when Mr Gladstone and the Queen tended to differ. Davidson, equally able but more ambitious, came to the Deanery at the early age of 33, and immediately succeeded to Wellesley's position in the royal confidence. Bishop Bell, Davidson's biographer, considered that 'in an uncommon degree' he was the royal pastor and teacher, and when a bishopric was offered to him in 1890 the Queen's first impulse was to forbid acceptance. The Dean went, but then frequently returned to preach before the Queen at Windsor.

The Queen's reliance on the two Deans symbolizes, however fortuitously, the re-emergence of the influence of St George's Chapel both locally and nationally. It had been famous and efficient in the reign of Charles II, probably its golden age; in the 18th century matins and evensong had continued to be sung daily, but deans and canons had been lax in attendance, and not until George III took his very great interest in the Chapel did life there revive. But this did not continue after his illness and death. By the 1830s things were at a low ebb. Services were not planned beforehand – just as the service was starting a choir boy would go up to the organ loft to ask the organist what he wanted sung.[15] And of 11 men choristers only four in fact were able to sing. Then, in 1835, George Elvey was made organist, and on his resignation 47 years later, he was followed by Walter Parratt ('less limited than any musician I know', was Benson's verdict), who remained until his death in 1924. Two organists of outstanding ability covered practically a century, they produced new standards. Once more St George's contributed an organist and choir for state occasions – for long the Chapel Royal staff had displaced them, even at Windsor. Elvey gained Victoria's regard, composing anthems for royal weddings as well as for matins, evensong, and, sign of the ecclesiastical times, for the eucharist. Parratt became still more active, taking part in two Jubilee services and two Coronation services. He was specially sent for by Edward VII and instructed to bring twelve choirboys in order to sing at the private services at Osborne when Queen Victoria died. Moreover, both organists regarded the town of Windsor as within their professional arena, as we shall see.[16] Elvey in the 1860s founded a Windsor and Eton Madrigal Society which, under Parratt, attained a membership of a hundred, including Princess Helena Victoria and her mother, Princess Christian. Practices were held every Saturday afternoon in the autumn and winter. Dr. Fellowes recalled that Parratt was a martinet about attendance and few dared to shirk.[17] Bach's B Minor Mass and the St John Passion became standard parts of the repertoire; madrigals were quite incidental.

Meanwhile, the constitution of the Chapel had been undergoing reform in two ways, each the result of Whig perception of inequality and inefficiency in church administration. There was wealth in the cathedrals, poverty in the parishes. The immediate effect on Windsor was that, by an Act of Parliament of 1840, the twelve canonries were progressively reduced to four, and deans were deprived of their sinecure and pluralist posts as Deans of Wolverhampton and Rectors of Great Haseley.[18] At the same time, minor canons were reduced in number from 13 to 4. A clerical post at St George's consequently became very much more demanding. Luckily, the quality of appointment rose more or less appropriately. We have already observed the two deans (not to mention the two organists). The canons included Frederick Anson, 1845 to 1885, who concentrated entirely on the administration of the chapel; the evangelical Lord Wriothesley Russell, 1840 – 1886, and his opposite, the tractarian member of the noble family of Earls of Devon, C.L. Courtenay, 1859 – 1894; and, most notable of all, the future King George V's tutor, Canon J. N. Dalton, 1885 – 1931, antiquary and administrator of a quite formidable type.[19] Links with the borough were strengthened. Dean Eliot in 1894 encouraged local branches of the YWCA and the Bible Society;[20] Canon Gee, himself previously Vicar of Windsor, gave lectures on history, handbills being distributed in the town; and members of the chapter were ready to take part in the services of the town's churches, however extreme, in either direction, the churchmanship.

In 1867 a further ecclesiastical reform took effect, which in fact over the following century or so critically weakened the power of the Chapel to minister at all widely, or to maintain efficiently what in fact is a quarter of Windsor Castle. By 1867 St George's admittedly was rich, perhaps the third richest church in the land. It owned manors, estates of about 12,000 acres in some 25 counties, and rectories.[21] In 1867 all this property was surrendered to the Ecclesiastical Commissioners in return for an assured income equal to the annual average for the three years, 1864 – 7. Inflation had not been heard of. It all seemed perfectly fair. But, a century later, after the First World War the sum agreed in 1867 of £14,000 no longer maintained even the staff, let alone the fabric. How much worse the position is today can be imagined.

Meanwhile, however, St George's was at the height of its fame. The Queen chose its once intended Lady Chapel as the Albert Memorial Chapel. The east end of the Choir was completely reconstructed as a further memorial to the Prince, with a good Clayton and Bell East Window, incidentally showing the Prince going about his visits to factories and academies, dressed in robes of the 14th century.[22] The marriage of the Prince of Wales to Princess Alexandra of Denmark took place in the Chapel in 1863, and the Registers of the Chapel list many notable royal marriages and funerals that followed. The registers culminate in the solemn service of 1901 when 'The Body of Her Most Excellent Majesty, Victoria by the Grace of God of the United Kingdom of Great Britain and Ireland Queen, Defender of the Faith and Empress of India, was conveyed from Osborne to Portsmouth on Friday February 1st 1901, and on the following day it was conveyed from Portsmouth to London and from London to Windsor into St George's Chapel, where a Funeral Service was held conducted by The Archbishop of Canterbury, The Bishop of Winchester and The Dean of Windsor.'[23]

References

1 D. Bennett, *King without a Crown* (1977), 67.
2 G. Rowell, *Queen Victoria goes to the Theatre* (1978), 47 – 65.
3 C. Woodham-Smith, *Queen Victoria 1819 – 61* (1972), 150.
4 ibid., 246 – 8.
5 ibid., 248 – 9.
6 ibid., 357 – 8.
7 Frogmore is described by Harwood, 274 – 286, by Oliver Headley *Round and About Windsor and District* (1949) 74 – 82; and in an official guide *The Royal Mausoleum, Frogmore*. The last is authoritative and has a plan of the mausoleum (1964, etc.).
8 Woodham-Smith, op.cit., 279, 430.
9 F. Ponsonby, *Recollections of Three Reigns* (1951), 48 – 9.
10 A. Ponsonby, *Henry Ponsonby* (1942), 82.
11 On the Windsor Tapestries see Gordon Cullingham's *The Royal Windsor Tapestry Manufactory 1876 – 1890*, 4 etc.
12 Princess Marie Louise, *My Memories of Six Reigns* (1956), 98.
13 Georgina Battiscombe, 'Gerald Wellesley; A Victorian Dean and Domestic Chaplain' RF St G (1963), 126 – 135, with a good portrait, plate 1.
14 G.K.A. Bell, *Randall Davidson* (1935), i, 64 – 123, who emphasizes Davidson's invigorating effect on the Chapel as a 'boy-Dean' in his thirties.
15 N. Wridgway, *The Choristers of St George's Chapel* (1980), 64; see also Lady Mary Elvey, *Life and Reminiscences of George Elvey, Knight*, (1894).

16 pp. 117 below.
17 E.H. Fellowes, *Memoirs of an Amateur Musician* (1946), 97.
18 S.L. Ollard, *Deans and Canons of Windsor* (1950), 23.
19 As yet there is no biography of this talented, if terrifying man; splendid anecdotes about him appear in Russell Thorndike's *Children of the Garter* (1937), a 'must' for any interested in the modern Chapel and choir.
20 A dean in the shadow of his brilliant predecessors, but notable in general Church Life; see Maurice Bond, 'Philip Frank Eliot' RF St G (1966 – 7) 314 – 331, and (1977 – 8), 381 – 394.
21 S. and M. Bond, 'The Chapter Acts of Windsor, 1430 – 1672' (1967). M St GC xlv – liii.
22 Maurice Bond, *Stained Glass at St George's Chapel* plate 23.
23 E.H.Fellowes and E.R. Poyser, *The Baptism, Marriage and Burial Registers of St George's Chapel Windsor* (1957), passim.

Victorian Windsor

(i) Urban Development

For the Borough of Windsor Victoria's reign had been as significant as for the Castle – in fact rather more so. Whereas the Castle in 1901 had very much the buildings and the number of inhabitants it had had at Victoria's accession, the borough was transformed in appearance – it ceased to be a mediaeval town – and its population grew considerably.

The beginning of decennial censuses in 1801[1] enables us to look at the latter development in some detail. In 1801 the enumerators found some 239 residents in the Castle; those of 1841 broke the Castle figures down into 230 for the Lower Ward, i.e. mainly St George's Chapel, 85 for the Upper Ward, and 44 for the 'Guard House'. A not very remarkable growth therefore from 239 to 359. But for the Parish of New Windsor there were 3,197 in 1801 and 7,528 in 1841: more than double. Finally the parish of Clewer had 1,695 in 1801 and 3,975 in 1841: again, more than double. By 1881 the total Borough population was 12,273; in 1901, 14,130. The Municipal Corporations Commission, noting continuing growth, commented that 'There is no considerable manufacture carried on in Windsor, and the increase of the town in size and apparent prosperity in the last few years, is to be attributed to the residence of the court.'[2]

The anomaly that what was in fact one town, New Windsor, included part of the neighbouring parish of Clewer was partly remedied by the Boundary Act of William IV. Under this Act the Clewer part of the town, northwards from Peascod and Thames Streets, joined the borough as the ward of 'Clewer Within', leaving the historic centre of Clewer and its surrounding fields as Clewer Without.[3] Much of the extended town remained unbuilt; the Boundaries Report on New Windsor noted (rather puzzlingly) that 'The principal part of the Borough of New Windsor is agricultural'; out of 2,500 acres, upwards of 1,700 are in possession of the Crown; and the parish of Clewer was 'principally of an agricultural character.' Yet, as we have seen, Windsor made little out of all its fields; if it was going to be the sort of extension to the Castle and supplier of services that seemed its destiny in the 19th century, some breaking of what survived of the old common field system was necessary. Until that occurred, rights of waste and pasture, and actual open field strips, prevented the construction of new roads and the growth of private estates of working-class houses. So Windsor and Clewer experienced what had been gradually happening throughout England over three centuries: Parliamentary enclosure. The first came in 1817 for Clewer.[4] Common fields in the triangle between 'Maidenhead Road', Clewer Hill Road and Winkfield

Villas in Osborne Road.

Road were finally organised into separate holdings – those to the south of Hatch Lane in the ownership of Richard Foster, and to the north, of Arthur Vansittart. The very wide area of common along Clewer Hill Road was reduced to the present narrow road, and 29 new separate properties were formed on the previous green. In the same way, the ever-widening green leading up to High Standing Hill produced 15 new privately owned properties. A similar enclosure process for New Windsor and Dedworth in 1819[5] turned the outlying Dedworth Field into 12 new tenements, and common rights within the Borough on Hatton Hill (where the Coach Station existed from 1933 to 1984), Spital Hill (the Osborne Road, Frances Road area) and other meadows were brought to an end. The era of unfettered freehold tenure had arrived.

A rather different, but almost equally important change in Windsor land tenure came in 1845. In 1843 the Commissioners of Woods and Forests had reported[6] that a large estate in Windsor was coming on the market which had 'long been the Property of the Keppel Family, and while in their Possession had never been used in any Manner which could be deemed objectionable to the Occupation of the Royal Residence; but as it was obvious that if it passed into other Hands in small Lots, there could be no security against Nuisances of various Descriptions'. The Crown acted, buying the estate 'after much Negociation' for £52,500. The Commissioners published a map showing that the Keppel estate so acquired consisted of Clayhall Farm on the Old Windsor side of the Long Walk, 16 acres north of Frogmore, practically all the lands between Sheet Street and the Long Walk, and the greater part of the land between Winkfield Road and Sheet Street, a broad swathe of properties across the east of the town, 287 acres in all. Passing into Crown ownership, they provided an outer bastion of protection for the Royal Family, and incidentally secured a substantial part of the town from cheap housing developments, since the subsequent Crown leases of areas not required for direct use by the Crown were carefully controlled.

A general result of this and other changes was that Victorian Windsor was divided into sociologically distinct areas: those for artisans, for tradespeople, and for gentry. The artisan area grew rapidly between 1830 and 1850 in the low-lying areas of Clewer Within, on the west. These had once included the goosefields, and were generically known (and still are) as the Goswells, pronounced 'Gozzles', then containing Windsor's worst and most insantiary houses between the Castle and the river. The tradespeople tended to live in the centre of the town, and the well-to-do gained Crown leases on the old Keppel Estate, part of which at the end of the reign attracted a quite remarkable number of inhabitants related to noble families for the only time in Windsor's history.

Leaving for the moment the social problems arising from this type of arrangement, a very much happier picture results from its architectural consequences. Victorian Windsor inherited and continued to build some rather nice houses, not in the Gothic style, but in a variety of Classical and Regency styles. Bath, consciously or unconsciously, was the exemplar, and

Goswells Road photographed in the 1960s, now the site of Ward Royal flats.

Windsor felt its way tentatively towards the unified terrace of domestic houses as it grew down Sheet Street towards the Park. A very high proportion of this building survives and can be enjoyed today.[7] For instance, in Kings Road there are Brunswick Terrace of c. 1800 of 13 houses in London stock brick; York Place of c. 1830, a terrace of buff brick; and Adelaide Terrace, 1831, a grand building with Ionic pilasters, entablature, pediment and the rest. All these flank the Long Walk and lead to the Great Park. Varied detail, such as balconies and verandahs make for minor variations, especially in the smaller houses, for instance Pucket's Close (no 24), standing between the terraces. Much simpler small houses, subsequently becoming shops in many cases, were built at right angles to the Sheet Street – Kings Road axis, along what was fittingly called Victoria Street, between 1820 and 1850. Practically 30 of these are now listed buildings. All have a simple classical regularity, no. 23 Victoria Street with 'good crisply moulded Ionic capitals'. And there are delightful early Victorian cottage-type houses in Gloucester Place and Adelaide Square, with humbler terraces in streets such as Grove Road.

The most coherent piece of early Victorian building was in the new ward of Clewer Within, but close to the main east – west route of Peascod Street and St Leonard's Road. This was laid out in the 1830s by the local builder and prominent councillor, James Bedborough.[8] When he died in 1860 the *Windsor Express* commented that Bedborough had done 'more than any other single individual to enhance the importance of this Borough'. Raymond South describes how this poor stone-mason aged 18 not only became a major building contractor but also constructed much of the main Great Western railway line and worked vigorously as a local (Whig) politician, twice serving as Mayor. His most stylish work was the small Clarence Crescent, with common gardens opposite; then with Clarence Road, Claremont Road, Dorset Road and Trinity Place filling up a symmetrical area. Vistas are closed by the tower and spire of Holy Trinity Church, a work of Edward Blore of 1842 – 4. As one wanders round this still very elegant district there is a variety of unobtrusive detail to admire, almost equalling the sub-Regency buildings by the Long Walk: flower guards, balconettes, pilastered porches. Early Victorian Windsor is still, without too much patching or infilling, being lived in and enjoyed.

Oddly enough, in spite of Windsor's considerable expansion under Victoria, there seems to have been a lull in building in the middle of the reign, say from 1850 to 1880, elsewhere the period of much high Victorian neo-Gothic building. Windsor has not a lot to show for this period. But there are the Windsor Almshouses in Victoria Street, of 1862,[9] gothicised polychrome brickwork, and the equally polychrome and rather splendid Riverside Station by Sir William Tite of 1851. This has a grand Reception Room for the Queen (now a private office) and a turret from which the look-out man could announce a royal arrival to the staff and dignitories on the platform. The Station is, in fact, Tudor Gothic, with depressed arched windows, and not excessively mediaeval. A long line of double doors enable the travellers to walk directly out of their compartments into the waiting carriages. The doors are high enough to permit the Household Cavalry to pass through without dismounting. VR and PA 1851 picked out in black brick identify this as a key Victorian building in Windsor.

Perhaps, however, the most worthy Victorian building is that sponsored by Prince Albert himself, not for the well-to-do traders or the gentry, but for the poor. This is the group of 48 simple red brick cottages ranged round a green in the centre of the town, the 'Prince Consort Model Cottages', built in 1855 not by Bedborough but by Henry Roberts, for the Royal Windsor Society under the Prince's direction, in order to provide salubrious housing for the poor. Gabled attics and dormers, pointed windows and doorways provide a mild neo-Gothic flavour.[10] Clearly a very successful form of architectural revivalism, it has recently been given a new lease of life by some discreet restoration, a nice counter-balance to the Bedborough estate.

Both Clarence Crescent and Prince Consort Cottages thus flourish today. What became a problem in Windsor for a century was the building done for the very poor. This was of course a national problem. Increase in population led to the provision of cheap dwellings on a large scale, crowded together, back to back, with no water supply and no sanitation – the labouring poor whether at Windsor or elsewhere in the new urban settlements were only washed thoroughly twice in their lives, at birth and at death. Tragically, as low-standard buildings multiplied, a new bacillic disease of cholera came to England from India, just at the same time, with a death rate varying from 5% to 50%. Cholera deaths occurred at Windsor in 1849, but similar diarrhoea-like deaths were frequently recorded. An outspoken Windsor surgeon, Mr Pearl, had bitterly criticised Bedborough for building houses for the poor with shallow wells near cesspools emptied only every month or so into an open ditch. Much of Windsor then undoubtedly stank. Bedborough, as Angus Macnaghten tells us, was thought by Pearl to be more interested in scarlet gowns for himself and his brethren, in venison and champagne, than in the good of the town. Mr Pearl had to resign in 1844; Alderman Bedborough went on to fame.[11] But criticism continued. The Crown in 1843[12] had wanted a joint drainage scheme with the Borough. The Council felt the matter should be left with the inhabitants, and John Secker, the Town Clerk, thought that the Council could not spend money on this sort of thing: it would be 'misapplying the Corporate Income to purposes for which it is no way liable.' However, the Public Health Act of 1848 authorised towns, where one tenth of the ratepayers petitioned in favour, to spend money to appoint

Inspectors of Nuisances, control drainage, and supervise slaughterhouses. Windsor did then take action. In 1850 the Council began to sit as a separate authority, the Windsor Board of Health, and the following year an underground system of sewers was begun. After a further quarter of a century,[13] in 1875, the sewage was delivered not into ditches and the Thames, but to a sewage farm on Ham Island in Old Windsor. In 1883 the regular removal of refuse to a field in Clewer, where it was used to fill hollows, began, and in 1884 the Board of Health started to seal up those wells in the town which were contaminated.

None of this quieted opposition. In 1858 even the Court Physician claimed that typhoid fever was epidemic in Windsor, and three years later, as we have seen, the death of Prince Albert was thought by some to have been caused by Windsor's lack of proper sanitation. Eventually in 1885 the leading medical journal, *The Lancet*, agitated for a special investigation of Windsor, and the government acted. Two inspectors came to the town, and after two years produced a report that must rank as one of the key documents in Windsor's archive.[14] The inspectors began with a little history. 'The gradual increase of population has necessitated a corresponding extension of house building. This has taken place within the borough, partly on the alluvial ground towards the river, below flood level, and partly on the sound gravel further south. Houses of the well-to-do class occupy the latter site; the low grounds are occupied by the cottages of the poor.' As a result, for instance during flood in 1852, water had stood in the Bier Lane (now River Street) houses for 17 days, reaching the tops of the kitchen grates. Without naming him, the Inspectors pinpointed the villain. They observed that 'It seems that South Place [on the lower ground] and Clarence Crescent [adjacent, but higher] were built by the same owner [i.e. Mr Bedborough], and that the sanitary interests of the former were sacrificed to the comfort and privacy of the latter.'

The Corporation blenched. It appointed an Inspector of Nusiances who they claimed, in their answer of 1889, was 'active and efficient'. A by-law was passed to insist on foundation in future being 68.8 feet above the O.S. level, i.e. above flooding. The Council coolly observed that 'the unsanitary areas in Windsor are not more numerous than might be expected', a strangely two-edged remark. In 1893 the Corporation began to consider the squalid piles of refuse disfiguring the river bank above the bridge. After much opposition, the bank was straightened and cleansed, and in 1903 the Alexandra Gardens were opened, a token, at least, that slum-life was on the way out.

However, this did not satisfy one Windsor resident, a radical and awkward councillor, William George Stoneham (an antiquarian bookseller who then lived at 53 Thames Street. He served as a County Councillor from 1898 to 1901 and then as a Borough Councillor fairly continuously from

Clarence Crescent.

1906 to 1927). In 1899 Stoneham publicly complained that the Council was suppressing the facts of Windsor's unhealthy life. Again government intervened, sending another Inspector, Dr Timbrall Bulstrode, who reported to the Board of Health[15] that he had not been welcomed by the leading Alderman when he visited the town on their behalf, though at the end of his visit, the same Alderman having toured with him the town's slums said he 'welcomed' an enquiry. Bulstrode got near the heart of Windsor's problem when he said that Windsor had no industry except two breweries and an aerated water factory. Hence, poor employment and low incomes. 100 cottages in the Goswells, known unfortunately as the Victoria Cottages (in Goswell Road, Denmark Street, Edward Square) were not suitable for habitation. He believed that the Corporation exercised its functions in a lukewarm and hesitating way; the Medical Officer of Health was 'too apologetic'; the Inspector of Nuisances 'disheartened'; the authorities lacked 'backbone' and were not free from blame.

This was not a particularly happy ending for the century at Windsor, but reforms gradually resulted. The Inspector took some test cases of neglect to court (where, however, they were promptly dismissed by the Magistrates); houses began to be demolished; and the Medical Officer of Health was made a supremo over the Inspector of Nuisances. Windsor was slowly emerging from the laissez-faire régime of the century. It had, perhaps as a result of the proximity of the Castle at several stages, because of direct Crown pressure, become a target for criticism. But Windsor's condition was that of all too many cities and towns. Dickens's novels and Disraeli's description of 'two Nations' were the negative side to the industrial growth and population increase that were the most notable features of Victorian England.

References

For a more detailed treatment of many aspects of Victorian Windsor, see Angus Macnaghten's invaluable *Windsor in Victorian Times* (1975) which deals in detail especially with personalities and buildings.

1 Raymond South analyses the census figures for 1801 – 1851 in his *The Fifth Hall Book of the Borough of New Windsor 1828 – 1852* (1974) see summary figures for 1801 – 1901 in VCH, ii, 241, 243.
2 The Commissioners Report is conveniently re-printed in TD, 623 – 631.
3 TD, ii, 621 – 3.
4 BRO.
5 BRO.
6 The 22nd Report of the Commissioners of Her Majesty's Woods, Forests, Land Revenues etc (1845). HC. 364, including plans on which this paragraph is based.
7 See Macnaghten op.cit., Pevsner, op.cit., and the schedule of Listed Buildings in Windsor in BRO.
8 R. South, op.cit., xxviii – xxix.
9 Macnaghten, op.cit., 50, 53; see BRO for the deed of settlement of 17 July 1852.
10 ibid, 40 – 41, 62, 70, 114. These have been recently most successfully modernised.
11 Macnaghten, op.cit., 25 – 6, 89, 100.
12 Mr South summarises the Council's action (or inaction) over public health between 1836 and 1850, op.cit., xxv – xxvi.
13 Events after 1850 are best studied in two records in the BRO: 'Report by Dr Hubert Airy and Mr Arnold Taylor in the Sanitary Conditions of New Windsor', Jan 1887, and the subsequent Report on this report, 20 November 1889; and 'Report by Dr H. Timbrall Bulstrode to the Local Government Board' of 1900.
14 BRO.
15 BRO.

(ii) Local Government

It is in some ways surprising that whether in Windsor or elsewhere, local authorities had not responded in the nineteenth century with greater alacrity to local needs. The Municipal Corporations Act of 1835 had made local government much more democratic than national government was to be for decades. Until 1835 the inhabitants of Windsor had had no direct say in the composition of the corporation. The Act of 1835 gave every ratepayer who had been resident for three years or more a vote, and throughout the century 'one occupier, one vote' was the rule. Women, however, were excluded until, in 1869, unmarried women with property qualifications were granted the local vote, and, in 1882, married women. In 1918 the non-property owning wives of male voters were admitted if they were over 30 years of age, and then, in 1928, this age was reduced to 21. Of course, those without property had no vote; the doctrine was that only those clearly owning wealth could properly control its use and distribution (this led councils rather naturally to value economy rather than public service). But in 1918 'paupers', as the propertyless were called, gained the local vote, and eventually, in 1945, all persons having the Parliamentary vote (which by then had soared beyond the local vote) received the local government vote, and, to make it entirely a local matter, in 1969 non-resident voters were excluded. It should be added, however, that, for much of the time, election to certain Local Boards was managed rather differently, in order to give extra weight to those paying heavier rates. Windsor people participated in all this democratisation, so that residents in the Goswells as well as those in Osborne Road took part in the election of councillors.

The new council of 1835 was relatively small, with 18 councillors only, representing the two wards of the Borough, but they then elected 6 aldermen.[1] The Council began, however hesitantly, as we have seen, to accept wider responsibilities than, in the main, managing Borough property and looking after the Bridge. In 1835 a Watch Committee was appointed to supervise constables,[2] and thereafter, in some sense, law and order in the town. A Finance Committee appeared, as well as what was to become the much more important General Purposes Committee.[3] The latter became all-powerful, an inner group of seniors, who dealt with such matters as highways, town planning, the gaol, water-supply, and in the 1840s, railway projects. All this meant the finding of larger sums of money. Rates were collected through the Churchwardens and Overseers of the Poor in the parishes of New Windsor and Clewer. This was the 'Borough Rate'. But the constables, as they grew into a quite large police force, proved so costly that a 'Watch Rate' had also to be levied regularly, whilst the old 'Poor Rate' continued to be gathered in separately.[4]

In 1850 the Councillors became ipso facto members of the new Windsor Board of Health, with power to supply houses with water-closets, pave streets, control slaughter-houses and regulate drainage (which thus disappeared from the agenda of General Purposes). Salaried officials such as the Surveyor and Inspector of Nuisances, a Treasurer, and a Rate Collector also came under their control. This development of 1850 has already been seen to have worked imperfectly. It was much disliked by the councillors. Henry Darvill complained in 1852 that 'The labours of the

Board of Health are twenty times greater than the labours of the Town Council and ought to be participated in by the whole body'.[5] Eventually in the twentieth century this became the case. Inhabitants began to elect councillors who took a more positive view of their duties. Councillor Stoneham whom we have already seen campaigning about the Goswells in 1899, had already appeared as a County Councillor in 1898; he lost that seat in 1901, but in 1906 was elected to the Borough Council and with some intervals continued a member until 1927, the year before his death, and by then he had ceased to be a lone voice. It is noticeable, however, that his last official act was to move on 12 October 1927 that some proceedings at the previous meeting were 'imperfect and illegal'.[6] There was no seconder. But after his death in the following January 1928, the Council stood for a short period in honour of his name, and its members had by then in many respects come to accept the relatively interventionist and protective attitude to local society that had been regarded with distaste when, perforce, the Health Committee had been formed in 1850, or, indeed when Dr Bulstrode came to Windsor in 1889.

References

1 *The Fifth Hall Book*, ed R. South (1974), xv.
2 op.cit., 18.
3 ibid.
4 op.cit., xxviii – xxiv.
5 op.cit., xxvi. Mr South prints the Minutes of Council meetings for the period to 1852. For further source material on the work of local administration see the documents noted in the *Handlist*, including General minutes of the Board, Finance and General Purposes Committes, BRO.
6 BRO.

(iii) The Railways

So far, the reformed and elected Council seems to have displayed little reforming zeal within its own area. But in one sphere, and that a vital one, it was enormously active and ultimately triumphant: that of transport. The railways came to Windsor in 1849 with the opening of a branch line from Slough by the London and Great Western Company, and of a separate branch line from Staines by the London and South Western Company. And, if some of Windsor's leading citizens had had their way Windsor would have had a railway even before Victoria had come to the throne. The Stockton and Darlington Railway had been finished in 1825, the Liverpool and Manchester Railway in 1830 and as Raymond South tells us in his definitive monograph, *Crown, College and Railways* (1978), local support for a 'London and Windsor Railway Company' was being organised by 1833.[1] The scheme was to have horsedrawn coaches on a track, which, in the November 1833 proposals, would approach Windsor from Colnbrook across the Thames, and then at high level would run along the Thames-side on its south to a terminus near Clewer Church. King William IV was said to have consented to such a line entering the town by Datchet Lane, crossing Thames Street and terminating 'at the back of the town'. Windsor's 'leading citizens' petitioned for leave to bring in a bill, but some local opinion veered towards an even more ambitious scheme: Windsor should be on a main line to the west; and thus 'a passing-place to the whole of the west of England'. Windsor's efforts were thwarted. A Great Western Act in 1835 authorised a line westwards through Slough (with no branch to Windsor) although only in 1840 was a station permitted even at Slough, so great were the fears of corruption of their pupils by Eton College.[2] An attempt in 1844 to have a 'Windsor Junction Railway' linking with Staines failed through opposition of the Crown.[3] Then later in 1844 an 'atmospheric' railway was planned. Cast iron pipes were to be laid between rails, and pistons projecting from the vehicles above fitted into the pipes and driven by atmospheric pressure. This idea had captivated the great engineer, I.K. Brunel, and two years later he did in fact have such a line, from Teignmouth to Newton Abbot, functioning, however inadequately.

No coal-fired locomotives, no smoke: it was an attractive idea, and local support was led by Robert Tighe, manager of a bank and a brewery in Windsor. Tighe opened a campaign on 17 October 1844 with a meeting at the White Hart Inn, when a company was formed to construct an atmospheric railway, with himself as Honorary Secretary, plus important figures such as Windsor's MP and James Bedborough as members of the Committee. The sympathy of the Crown was sought by a plan to make the royal estates round Windsor Castle as insulated as they could be by closing the Old Windsor road across Frogmore and substituting a road far to the south, thus giving the Queen absolute privacy on the Frogmore estate. By 8 votes to 4 the Town Council petitioned Parliament in favour.[5] The railway, however, would have to cross part of Eton College playing fields; Eton boys would be tempted to throw stones at the trains. Again, Eton triumphed over Windsor. The Commons Committee decided against the Atmospheric Railway.

This decision left Windsor councillors in a dilemma; there was a main line to the north, the Great Western; another to the south, the South Western. With which of the great companies should townspeople ally? Public meetings that became disorderly, a local poll and then a grand parliamentary battle saw both schemes steadily advance during 1847 and 1848, allied with a 'Town Approaches Bill' picked up from Robert Tighe's proposals in order to placate the Crown authorities. By the end of 1849 Windsor had attained two branch lines, and (by 1851) two railway stations, one on riverside, the other under the walls of the Castle. The South Western

Company paid the Commissioners of Woods and Forests £60,000 'towards the expense of constructing the said roads and bridges and of widening and improving Thames Street and High Street Windsor' and the Great Western Company paid the Crown £25,000 for the surrender of Crown land in Windsor and Eton. In addition, three new roads and two new bridges were authorised.

On many counts the railway decisions of 1849 were crucial in Windsor's history. Firstly, Windsor became suburban rather than provincial. After 1 December 1849, Windsor residents could catch an 8.5 train and arrive at Paddington in an hour, or, an 8.45 train and arrive at Waterloo at 9.40.[6] Commuting began and, ever since, many Windsor people have led a split life, working in London and sleeping in Windsor. They have additionally had the great advantage of shopping in London, enjoying its concerts, exhibitions and sporting events. Never very conscious of its 'county' status, Windsor turned even more than previously away from the county town of Reading and became London-oriented and, to some extent, cosmopolitan.

Secondly, the tourism established in the 14th century suddenly became very big business indeed. Where coaches could only bring dozens, railway trains brought hundreds, and as the British railway net-work evolved, excursions could come on day-outings from distant cities in the Midlands. Until the development of motor cars before the First World War and of 'charabancs' in the 1920s, the railways were the nation's link with Windsor (and *vice versa*). On 23 November 1849 the royal household travelled by train from Windsor for the first time, and thereafter monarchs, ambassadors and cabinet ministers habitually made use of the two Windsor railway branch lines, which from time to time became key elements in great public ceremonies such as Royal Funerals. The railways vastly increased Windsor's national status.

Thirdly, and this must have been in the councillors' minds from the 1830s onwards, the many transient railway visitors needed Windsor's 'service industries'; they bought souvenirs, guidebooks, meals, drinks in the town, increasing the prosperity of the leading Windsor tradespeople. Not until the 1920s was there any serious demand for local industry; the drapers, grocers, stationers and innkeepers of Windsor were being kept very reasonably employed.

Lastly, 1849 dramatically changed the appearance of Windsor. It gave Windsor (in two stages) its best Victorian buildings: Sir William Tite's South Western Railway Station of 1850, with diapered bricks and a fine royal waiting room partly imitated from Henry VII's Chapel at Westminster Abbey; and the late Victorian Great Western Station re-constructed in 1897, with luxurious accommodation for the Royal Family.[7] The somewhat squalid tenements in the Castle ditch were demolished, revealing the splendid 13th century western walls of the Castle.

Park Street was terminated at the Long Walk and the mile-distant Albert Road substituted to the south for the Frogmore Road to Staines. The process, started by Edward III, by which the Castle acquired a large area of private estates, was completed, and the Borough became essentially a fairly tightly confined area bounded by royal estates and the river. This may have been cramping by comparison with the time when Windsor people had once enjoyed property entirely surrounding the Castle Hill; but it saved 20th century Windsor from the unplanned and overwhelming suburban exploitation suffered by many ancient towns and villages west of London.

It might not be unreasonable to add one further result of 1849. Robert Tighe's activities on behalf both of the railways and royal privacy led him to employ a brilliant young barrister, James Davis, to search as many historic records as were available in order to compile a reliable local history, not merely as a *pièce justicatif* for an Atmospheric Railway, but as a solid contribution to knowledge. Davis laboured for 13 years, and in 1858 there appeared the *Annals of Windsor* (Tighe and Davis), a brilliant selection of source material, still the best work on Windsor, and the starting point for the present book as well as for most other Windsorian studies.[8] 1849 was a key date for both the future and also the past of Windsor.

A footnote to the story of the railway history of Windsor needs to be added. One of the great railway engineers of the century had his home in Windsor – or, rather in what was then the village of Clewer. Daniel Gooch (1816 – 1889) at the age of 21 had been appointed Superintendent of the Great Western Railway on the recommendation of Brunel. Thereby he shared credit for that company's great successes as well as responsibility for its ultimate failures over the atmospheric and broad gauge system. Gooch served the company for the rest of his life except for the extraordinary year 1864 – 5 when he turned to the still greater task of laying the cables crossing the Atlantic which made telegraphic communication with America possible.

Chairman of the GWR from 1865, he was also director of many other railway companies, Member of Parliament for Cricklade between 1865 and 1885, Deputy Lieutenant for Wiltshire, Justice of the Peace for Berkshire and created a Baronet in 1866; one of the notable Victorians. His diaries make clear that what helped to keep him going in the midst of never-ceasing political and engineering conflicts was his home at Clewer Park, an estate lying immediately behind Clewer Village and Mill Lane, on the Maidenhead side. He went there in 1859 and stayed for the rest of his life. Ten years after he arrived, he still felt that Clewer Park with elms, cedars and mill stream was 'very beautiful'.

The Foresters had their fete in his estate; Gooch sat on the Bench in the Guildhall at Quarter Sessions; in the 1860s he replaced the irregular line of cottages in the west side of Mill Lane, Clewer, with the houses still there

Part of the Tussaud's Royalty and Empire Exhibition at the Windsor Central (W.R.) Station. Courtesy of the Thames and Chilterns Tourist Board.

today, and his coat of arms appears on one of them. He now lies buried in Clewer churchyard. His long residence at Clewer Park gives the town a personal link with railway history over and above the more immediate and parochial story of the two branch lines to Windsor, and adds significantly to the roll of talented and creative men of the Borough.

References

1 op.cit., 15 – 18.
2 Eton's ultimately ineffective opposition is decisively documented by Mr South. op.cit., 20 – 23.
3 op.cit., 36 – 39.
4 op.cit., 38, 83 – 4; see also M.F. Bond 'A Century of Windsor History 1858 – 1958', BAJ, vol. 57 (1959), 34 – 51, passim; and TD, i, xiii.
5 op.cit., 43.
6 See the timetables printed, op.cit., 122 – 3.
7 The original GWR station was timber-built to Brunel's design. In 1897 Queen Victoria's Diamond Jubilee was commemorated by the construction of a splendid brick, glass and steel building, with a royal waiting room out-rivalling the LSWR accommodation. Although a shuttle-line to Slough still serves the 'Western' station, the greater part of the station houses the Tussauds Royalty and Empire Exhibition depicting the arrival of a royal train in 1897 (an Achilles class locomotive with a replica of Queen Victoria's personal carriage, the 'Royal Day Saloon' stands by the arrival platform).
8 cf M.F. Bond, op.cit., n.4, above.
9 On Gooch's life, see R.D. Wilson, *Sir Daniel Gooch, Memoirs and Diary* (1972), passim, and Dictionary of National Biography under 'Gooch'; also Denis Shaw, *Here Lies . . .* (May 1982), 8, where Clewer Park is noted as previously the home of the Hon. Henry Ashley, brother to the reformer Lord Shaftesbury. The house was in an Italianate early Victorian style. A housing development now replaces the mansion.

(iv) The Churches

Mayors, Aldermen and Councillors were obviously quite powerful men, whether they used their powers adequately (in helping to bring the railways to Windsor, for instance) or not. Yet in Victorian Windsor it may be that still more significant at various moments were the clergy. Inhabitants did not attend council meetings, but whether shopkeeper or artisan, probably one member of most families went fairly regularly to church or chapel. Vicars and Rectors and Ministers, not to mention Deans and Canons, were important people in Windsor. It is noticeable, for instance, that the *Windsor Express* started its local news with a statement as to who was in residence that week as Canon at St George's.

This was mid-Victorian. At the beginning of the century the established religion was not flourishing. Anglicans outside the Castle had only two buildings, St John Baptist in the High Street and St Andrew's at Clewer. By 1900, however, there was a multiplicity of churches and chapels, buttressed

The Congregational Church in William Street, which was demolished in the 1970s.

by a system of church schools that in the 1980s remain powerful and highly significant.

Congregations dissenting from the Established Church, however, had long been active. The Commonwealth period of 1649 – 1660 must have left behind many 'independents', who no more than outwardly and irregularly conformed to the parish church, and by 1676 there were 115 dissenters out of 1,025 adults in Windsor.[1] The foremost leaders in the opposition to the restored established church in 1660 had been the Quakers,[2] and a severe test of 1662 inflicted penalties (up to transportation) for those attending Quaker meetings. But the Quakers were not suppressed – of all dissenting bodies we know most about them, in any case, as it was they who kept the best records. Original records survive of the Quakers in eastern Berkshire from 1668 onwards. An early entry in a Minute Book, ominously records how 'came the officers and souldiers into the house of Thomas Davie, where he with his family and friends were peaceably mett together to waite upon the Lord'. Seven were taken before the Governor of Windsor Castle and then before the Mayor of Windsor, who conveyed them to gaol at Reading. A later entry, for 31 November 1733, shows 7 Friends at their meeting in Windsor. They considered an 'abstract' of Friends sufferings and set on foot an enquiry into the suitability of a proposed marriage for a Friend who sought the Meeting's Certificate. And they collected 6s.6d. amongst themselves.

A burial ground was acquired by 1698 between what is now King's Road and the Sheet Field (ie the Long Walk). This was still in use in 1826 – 7, as bills for work there still testify, but the Windsor Monthly Meeting, established in 1668, was demolished in 1755 and united to the Reading Meeting. Today there are still meetings for Windsor Friends but usually not in the town, and of course, only a short distance away is the most famous of all Quaker meeting houses in the world: the Friends Meeting House at Jordans (east of Beaconsfield) which was built as such in 1688. There still can be seen the headstone of the burial place of William Penn, founding father of the State of Pennsylvania, USA.

When in 1844 the Rev John Stoughton, himself a Congregational Minister, compiled a history of Windsor he perhaps naturally claimed that the Independents (by then 'Congregationalists') were the oldest of Windsor's dissenting communities.[4] They had met first in a building in Peascod Street called 'the Hole in the Wall'; then they moved to 'an inconvenient place of worship' in the midst of the Bier Lane slums. In 1832 a new era for them began with the construction of a 'fine, proud chapel' (in Pevsner's words) constructed by Jesse Hollis, in William Street. This, sadly, has just been pulled down, and a smaller, and obviously more convenient brick multi-purpose church substituted. But Pevsner's celebration of one of Windsor's notable buildings, as he saw it in 1966,

The Baptist Church in Victoria Street.

should be recorded in full: 'Still undisturbed classical. Yellow brick, three bays with a three bay pediment. Tuscan porch. Arched upper windows.'[5] A building as fine as the Bedborough estate villas and eloquent witness to the confidence of Windsor nonconformity.

Its counterpart round the corner, in Victoria Street, is the still partly Baptist Church, 'equally pround and equally classical',[6] with members working quite closely with the Congregational, with gospel messages and temperance movements deriving joint support from them. Tragically, the rear part of the church building was demolished in 1984 following the collapse of the ceiling.

John Wesley's message had long before led to the establishment of a third nonconformist group. Jean Kirkwood in her *The Methodist Church, The Centenary Story*,[7] quoting from John Wesley's Journal, refers to the entry of 26 September 1738: 'I declared the Gospel of Peace to a small company in Windsor'. There were 13 more visits by Wesley up to 1750 – in the last year he considered his congregation at Windsor 'large and extremely still and attentive a very few persons excepted'. No more is known until, in 1826, a young soldier attended a prayer meeting held in Windsor by another soldier. A chapel seems to have existed in Bier Lane by 1820, and then in 1836 a new chapel was built, where nos. 107 – 8 Peascod Street now are, with the support, it is interesting to note, of the Duke of Cambridge, Sir Jeffry Wyatville and the Vicar of Windsor. After 40 years the Methodist congregation moved to the present Methodist church in Alma Road, and in 1888 a Christian Workers' Association was formed which, *inter alia*, formed a 'button-holing brigade' which would 'proceed to Oxford Road and neighbourhood to compel the wanderer to come in'. Mission work was done in the barracks, and a special part of the Chapel was labelled 'Military'. Clearly the services were well attended, the boys being put in the galleries, where inevitably they were disorderly.

This variety and strength of Protestant witness in the town is not unexpected in view of the earlier history of Puritan and anti-Laudian sympathies. But the ecclesiastical spectrum had been for long still wider. At the beginning of the 18th century Father John Chapman Vere St Leger, a Jesuit, lived at Spital; and in 1727 a Portuguese priest, living under a layman's alias, died in Windsor.[8] Mass was obviously being said in private houses, but there is no definite location known until 1810, when the house known as the Hermitage at Clewer Green had a family chaplain, and a room there was known as the chapel of St John. Soon after the 1830s collections were begun to build a separate and more public church. Fears were expressed that this might be regarded as 'an aggression on the stronghold of the Court' – fears rightly waived aside by the Windsor priest. But money did not flow in, and only in 1868 was the present church of St Edward the Confessor dedicated in Alma Road, by Archbishop

Manning (later the Cardinal of Westminster). In 1889 the distinguished Canon Longinotto came as parish priest, spending 47 years at Windsor, extending the church, playing a vigorous part as a member of the Windsor Education Committee, building a school behind the church, and entering into the life of the town in many ways, not least by his lectures at the Albert Institute on Italian art and architecture.

Windsor thus was by no means the preserve of the established church in the 19th century. Even as late as the 1840s the life of the two Windsor Anglican parishes was distinctly lacklustre. Neither incumbent lived in the town, each leaving the work to a curate, and of the two incumbents, one chose to live in a Piccadilly hotel, coming down for Sundays, marriages and funerals. What made things rather worse was that each parish church was too small and almost derelict. The story of Clewer comes a little later, but so far as Windsor church was concerned the first difficulty was that its system of large pews was so designed, as the *Windsor Guide* of 1793 noted 'as to exclude the majority of the inhabitants from attending Divine Service'. The whole structure, moreover, after centuries of inefficient patching, was becoming unsafe, worship 'perilous'.[9] So the tower was removed, and then, between 1820 and 1822 the rest of the building, the present church being constructed to replace it by C. Hollis. In 1870 his rectangular box-like structure was given the much more attractive eastern chancel by S. Teulon. Galleries had been constructed, and a full church probably meant some 1,700 in the congregation. In passing, it should be added that elegant monuments were transferred from the earlier structure, among them two of the 17th century by Edward Marshall, and two of the 18th by Peter Scheemakers. The Victorian building also acquired most beautiful railings for its south chapel by Grinling Gibbons, brought from the dismantled chapel royal in the Upper Ward, and a striking oil-painting of the Last Supper by Francis de Cleyn, previously hung in St George's Chapel as reredos. And, for those of the parish, equally important, clergy of higher calibre came to serve it, starting with Isaac Gosset (Vicar, 1821 to 1855) with his genius of a curate, George Augustus Selwyn, subsequent founder of the church in New Zealand, and today commemorated by the college named after him in Cambridge.[10]

But even a church in High Street for between one and two thousand, and some able clergy, were hardly a complete answer for a population of 10,000 or more – and one, moreover, which had a substantial garrison element. The problem concerned both Windsor and Clewer, perhaps the latter more, since Clewer's boundaries came to the centre of the expansion area of Windsor. Consequently Clewer parish was twice divided during the century, with new parish churches appearing, that of Holy Trinity in 1842 and of St Stephen in 1872; whilst each of the parent churches acquired district churches, Windsor gaining All Saints in 1864, and Clewer, the small

Holy Trinity Church.

St Agnes at Spital in 1874[11] and the rather larger All Saints, Dedworth in 1863. Holy Trinity, in its turn, built a district church of St Saviour in River Street (1876). When Victoria came to the throne Anglicans had two places of worship; by her Diamond Jubilee, there were eight.

The place of these churches in the life of Victorian Windsor was considerable. Firstly, Holy Trinity church served as the focus of the new Bedborough estate and it also caught the public imagination. It became the garrison church, and until the last war, each Sunday, military parades led by bands marched to Holy Trinity, the soldiers in their scarlet filling the galleries. After return to barracks, what amounted to brass band concerts were given to the public. Windsor ladies bought their best hats for Holy Trinity services; it was the fashionable church. But it was much more than that. Holy Trinity parish had not only soldiers, it had slums. When the 1849 cholera epidemic came to Windsor the parish collected money, opened soup kitchens, started reading-rooms and later, on the appointment of a robust and challenging rector, Arthur Robins (1873 to 1899), led a public campaign against what he described as the total lack of sanitation, the polluted wells, the rat-ridden tenements, of his Bier Lane, and Goswells parishioners. Miss Tower, herself the daughter of Robins's much-loved successor, Canon Henry Tower, very fairly remarks that Robins did not allow the members of his congregation to take refuge in comfortable ignorance of what was occurring in the homes of the less fortunate.[12] Robins was Windsor's radical parson; he made the headlines in the national newspapers and was accorded the dignity of a 'Spy' cartoon. Robins also planted in the midst of the slums the church of St Saviour, which, quite unendowed, was supported by contributions from the Holy Trinity congregation, until as part of slum clearance in the 1920s, St Saviour's was demolished along with the slums themselves.[13]

Robins spoke and worked from a distinctively Evangelical position. Holy Trinity during the 19th century became to some extent, a 'Low Church' centre though never a doctrinaire or kensitite one. But it so happened that in the other half of the old parish of Clewer things were moving in the opposite direction. The High Church movement which began at Oxford in 1834 had as one of its most active disciples Thomas Thellusson Carter, who was appointed Rector of Clewer in 1844, resigning in 1879 but then remaining in Clewer as Warden of the Convent he had founded until his death in 1901 – a formidable continuity of influence of nearly 60 years. His achievements were diverse, controversial, and, on a general view, of even international importance.[14] Firstly, Canon Carter found Clewer church in the 1840s nearly as ruinous as Windsor church had been in the 1820s. Destruction was a real possiblity. But by 1860 the Nave of the church had been thoroughly restored (the somewhat 'bastard' type of Norman pillar on the north is Carter's); a strange pointed arch now to be seen between the Tower and the Nave is not an odd type of 12th century 'Gothic', but, as Father Shaw has recently suggested a piece of Victorian reconstruction. But the main church was preserved, and can claim to be the most interesting and historic building outside the Castle in Windsor today. Much of the detail of the Clewer parish story can be traced in the permanent historical exhibition now maintained in the house at the lych-gate.

Then, like Robins, Carter faced the problems of Windsor destitution. In this he had the help of two remarkable women, Maraquita Tennant and Harriet Monsell. He began efforts to care for 'girls from the worst quarter of a garrison town'. A House of Mercy where they could live was built in Hatch Lane in 1849. A sisterhood of nuns to care for them began work in 1851, and by the end of the century there were some 47 linked institutions throughout the world, supervised from Clewer by Carter and his Sisters of Mercy. Some of these foundations were in Windsor, educational and charitable, others in Oxford, Pimlico, Soho, Torquay, Calcutta, Darjeeling and New York. Windsor gained a boarding school for girls (St Stephen's College) and then, in 1882, St Stephen's High School, mainly for day-girls and very much part of the Windsor scene until its closure in 1934. There

The Rev. Arthur Robins.

were also National and Intermediate mixed schools. This educational complex was nearer the centre of Windsor than either St Andrew's Church or the House of Mercy (generally known now as the Convent). The complex focussed on the new church and parish of St Stephen's, Clewer, which received their first incumbent, Father Nicholas, in 1871. This social work at Clewer came to the attention of Mr Gladstone, and the prostitutes he found in the streets of London frequently were received and looked after by the Sisters at Clewer convent.

But Carter, like Robins, was controversial, if in a different fashion. Mass vestments, incense, the circulation of translated Roman Catholic books of devotion (more than a hundred separate titles), and the appearance in the streets of the town of priests in soutanes and birettas, and of veiled nuns caused a good deal of protestant misgiving. What was happening to the established church under the very walls of the Castle in which its Royal Defender lived? Carter considered that the church must absorb into itself whatever could be helpful to devotional life which it had used in the Middle Ages and still survived on the Continent. Many disagreed with him and his Anglo-Catholic brethren. In 1877 the Public Worship Regulation Act, which gave effect to Protestant anger, enabled a law suit to be entered against Carter for 'ritual excesses' concerning the position of the priest at the altar, the use of candles and of mass vestments (which had certainly alienated the Clewer gentry, but which are all today commonplace). The outcome was not a verdict, but resignation. Carter left the rectory and concentrated for the remainder of his life on Wardenship of the Convent, with some hundreds of sisters in up to 40 convents scattered throughout the world. After Carter's death the net-work tended to fall apart. Social and educational services were increasingly provided by national authorities, but the impetus given by Carter to the Catholic movement in the Church of England becomes more rather than less significant as time passes, and, at Windsor, Sisters continue to live in the Convent buildings, having acquired in 1881 what Pevsner describes as an 'astonishingly grand and lavish' chapel, one of the distinguished monuments in this country of High Victorianism.[15]

References

1 Raymond South, *Royal Castle, Rebel Town* (1981), 99.
2 Those in Windsor are mentioned in South, op.cit., 98.
3 BRO. Burial ground deeds; bills.
4 J. Stoughton, *Windsor: A history and description of the Castle and Town* (1862 ed.), Quoting from his original *Windsor in the Older Time* (1844), 190.
5 N. Pevsner, *Berkshire* (1966), 301.
6 ibid.
7 op.cit., (1977).
8 On Roman Catholic Windsor, see *Church of St Edward, King and Confessor Windsor 1868 – 1968* (1968).

Interior of Clewer Church.

9 Harwood, 347 – 8, where the church is described as 'little better than a private chapel for the Mayor, the Corporation, and their friends'.
10 TD, passim, prints extracts from the Church Wardens' Accounts of the 17th and 18th centuries. BRO holds an extensive archive for the parish by the Rector, Rev D.N. Griffiths, PSA. See also *A few facts concerning Windsor Parish Church and All Saints's Church* by H.F.G. (Woodford), n.d. (c. 1900).
11 St Agnes is strictly the private (proprietory) chapel of successive Rectors of Clewer. Its active lye as a 'district' church has been recently described by Valerie Bonham in a well-researched book, *In the Midst of the People* (1983) – with some splendid illustrations.
12 Cicely Tower, *The Story of Holy Trinity Church, Windsor* (n.d.)
13 Robins also championed the cause of soldiers – why, for instance, did a Windsor hotel refuse to serve a soldier in uniform; why were soldiers punished with brutal floggings? Robins saw himself very much as the soldiers' padre. There is more about this splendid man in Alfred Capper *A Rambler's Recollections and Reflections* (1915), chapter 14 'The Soldiers' Bishop'.
14 The description of Carter's work is derived from *The life and letters of TT Carter* ed. W.J. Hutchings, 3d ed. (1904), especially pp. 34 (church reconstruction); 41 (St Stephen's Church); 83 (Clewer House of Mercy); 150 (the Clewer Case); and 322 (Wardenship of the Convent). See also W. Elwell, *History of Clewer* (1928); R.L. Bull, *The Church of St Stephen* (1974); T.T. Carter, *Harnet Monsell* (1884); and P.F. Anson, *The Call of the Cloister* (1958 ed.), 'Commands of St John the Baptist', at pp. 304 – 317. M.F. Bond described the now demolished Clewer Rectory in BAJ (1963 – 4), vol d, pp. 79 – 82. Mary Clewer parochialia are shown in the Clewer History Museum (descriptive catalogue available).
15 This was the work of Henry Woodyer, Pevsner op. cit., 305.

(v) The Arts

If religion included a very positive contribution to the social conditions of the poor in Windsor, there were many other developments in Victorian Windsor which, if mainly for the fairly prosperous, also made life generally more interesting and creative. This was in the field of the arts. Windsor was well-placed for this sort of creativity. With Eton College across the river, and the Royal Household and St George's Chapel in the Castle, the Borough had both patrons and performers of distinction to hand. Although in many ways, College, Castle, Chapel and Borough have gone their own separate ways, the closest co-operation for long has been and remains in what can be summed up as cultural life.

The marked development of this was Victorian; but roots lay far in the past. Music had obviously been performed professionally in the chapels of Eton and St George's since the Middle Ages. Plays were enacted in the Castle, and as we have seen, St George's choirboys appear to have been used as actors in Shakespeare's time. Education had had its origins not only in humble grammatical teaching by Windsor priests, but also in somewhat more ambitious efforts by the Masters of the Choristers in the Castle, and above all in the wealthy foundation of Eton College, to which a certain number of local boys seem to have gone as scholars. So far as entertainment was concerned, travelling mummers, local feast day merriment, Bachelors Acre revels, parish perambulations and civic feasts had all contributed to some alleviation of the drudgery of daily routine.

A key date as far as entertainment is concerned is 1706. In that year an actor named Yates, we are told by the theatrical historian, R.P. Mander,[1] 'opened a booth in the old town [Windsor] where, if tradition is to be believed, Mrs Susan Carol, a widow, better known under her surname of Outlivre, assumed with complete success the heroic role of Alexander the Great.' Her husband, Joseph, was Queen Anne's principal cook. We do not know where the booth was, but by 1778 there was a small barn in a field at the foot of Peascod Street (or perhaps, St Leonard's Road) known as 'The Theatre Royal', and its playbills are still preserved in the British Museum. In 1793, no doubt with active royal encouragement, the theatre moved to High Street, to the site of the present Constitution House. George III, Queen Charlotte and their family were regular patrons. 'One side of the lower tier of Boxes was reserved for him and his entourage. The King and Queen were provided with capacious armchairs and given playbills printed on silk' (which other playgoers subsequently fought for as souvenirs). Some of the actors were from London – in 1827 the light comedian and manager was from Drury Lane and a fellow actor had made his reputation at the Old Vic (then the Royal Coburg); in 1832 the great Edmund Kean was a guest actor. Plays varied from adaptations, incredibly, of Wycherly, to Shakespeare and also to tragedies now long forgotten. Audiences, perforce, were small, as the theatre was minute. The King, from his box, could have shaken hands with any of the townsmen in the pit. But the illness of the King after 1810, the persistent hostility of Eton College masters, who feared their pupils' corruption, and the action of a group of dissenters in capturing the lease of the theatre building in 1815 ended the High Street Theatre. Ironically it became the Congregational Chapel, until the grander building in William Street appeared.

Windsor Theatre did not die, however. In 1815 a new Theatre Royal opened in Thames Street and continued until a disastrous fire in 1908, when the present Theatre replaced it on the same site. The Theatre remained 'Royal' and is a Patent Theatre, licensed directly by the Lord Chamberlain because it is situated in a town in which the Sovereign resides – with a theoretical right to a twenty-four hour licence for its bars. And during both the former and the present Sovereigns' reigns the Royal Family and their guests have brought active royal patronage back to it.

The Theatre in fact flourished. Eton College lifted the rigorous ban on any acting in term time when its old Statutes were repealed, and the Lord Chamberlain did not support the Headmaster when in 1869 he tried to have a performance stopped, 'hearing that a number of Etonians were in the audience'. For a short time in the 1930s the tradition of two centuries was interrupted when the Theatre became a cinema. But in 1933 John Counsell gave the first production of 'Clive of India' in the Theatre, subsequently founded the present 'Windsor Repertory Company', and with his distinguished actress wife, Mary Kerridge, has continued to maintain Windsor Theatre at a high level of artistic success where notable actors and future London successes made their début.[2] Often when Windsor is mentioned, after the Castle its Theatre is likely to be the next feature of its life on which comment is made.

The Theatre is professional; to a local resident opportunities for amateur performance have been equally significant, and these were very much a Victorian innovation as a part of a broad range of amateur activity in the arts, probably unequalled in any other small town in the country. Mervyn Bruxner has suggested that a key moment was in the year before Victoria's succession, in December 1836, when 'a young man of 20 called George Job Elvey, who had been recently appointed Organist of St George's Chapel, Windsor, invited about 40 people to his house and made them sing some of 'The Messiah'[3]. On 24 January 1837 these 40, with 50 players, performed part of the work in public rooms in High Street. So began the Windsor and Eton Choral Society. Eton, in the person of its 'Mathematical Assistant', the Rev Stephen Hawtrey, joined in, and the tripartite union of St George's Chapel, Eton and the Borough, that has continued ever since, is one of the most striking examples of the way in which the three very separate and disparate bodies have worked together to the benefit of the neighbourhood. By 1844 the Society was able to perform concerts as elaborate as that at the Mathematics School at Eton on 25 January. It inevitably included selections from 'Messiah', but there were also songs and madrigals by Thomas Morley and John Wilbye, together with an 'Ode composed on the Birth of the Prince of Wales' by Elvey. Elvey, of course, involved his own Lay Clerks in the performances; in 1847 Prince Albert became Patron. A generation later, Elvey, now Sir George, reported how 'well and fashionably attended' a concert had been, though he was more critical of the singers attendance at weekly practices; 'very small attendance', 'quite tolerable', he carefully commented in his private note book. St George's Chapel and Windsor Guildhall were the normal venues for the Victorian concerts until the Albert Institute was opened in 1880. This had acoustic qualities, 'peculiarly adapted for concerts.' Princess Christian succeeded Prince Albert as Patron, and by the end of the century members of the royal family were taking part in concerts, and it was no doubt their influence that enabled the Institute to borrow cushioned chairs for the front seats from the Lord Chamberlain. Dr Lloyd, Organist at Eton, Sir Walter Parratt of St George's, and even Sir George Grove, Director of the Royal College of Music (of enduring *Grove's Dictionary* fame) lent support after Elvey's resignation in 1882. By the present century a new grouping, more municipal in character, had taken over. In the 1930s, for instance, Alderman Sir Frederick Dyson was Chairman; the Vicar of Windsor, President; and a keen young master from the Boys' County School, E.H. Austin, was Secretary. Minor Canon M.C. Everitt was Conductor – who, having heard Everitt's conducting Elgar's *Dream of Gerontius* in Eton School Hall will forget the tremendous moment when Gerontius's soul met God, to an enormous orchestral crescendo.

Choirs on this massive scale needed orchestral accompaniment; and middle-class Victorians were nothing if not ardent pianists and violinists in their own homes. In 1883, 13 people met at the Albert Institute to form an Orchestral Society 'for the performance of Classical music'.[4] By 1897 there were 56 members, each of whom had to prove himself in at least one instrument. In 1899 members were accepted for instance who played the oboe, the violin and the viola. An annual concert was given to support the Albert Institute – and the music ranged widely, including Max Bruch's *Romance for Violin*, as well as Beethoven, Saint-Saens and Bach. St George's again helped in the person of Sir Walter Parratt the Conductor, and Eton provided Dr C.H. Lloyd when Parratt retired. The Madrigal Singers (yet another musical group) and the Choral Society were supported by the orchestra; the Albert Institute was firmly established as an important, if local, musical centre.[5]

The first idea of this 'institute' had been educational. The poorer classes needed the chance to obtain education which they had missed or not been offered at the National and British Schools. In 1835 a 'Literary, Scientific and Mechanics Institute for the Propagation of Literature and Music' was set up, clearly aiming at providing both instruction and entertainment. Angus Macnaghten[6] notes the 'very large fetes, which included cricket matches, amusements of many kinds for children and adults, and dancing', together with an 'annual winter soirée' beginning in the Guildhall in 1857, and an exhibition of 'photographs, lithographs and galvanophotography' in its own premises – the hunger of semi-literate poorly paid people for apparently quite esoteric subjects such as mineralogy, geology and the newer sciences was a local phenomenon as well as a national one in mid-Victorian days. The Mechanics' Institute was quite long-lived; outings to Margate, lectures, and 'entertainments' were still being organised in 1879, and at one moment it contemplated buying the Theatre. A better idea came when it was felt that a proper commemoration in the town of Prince Albert, who died in 1861, was appropriate. A new centre for the whole cluster of voluntary cultural societies was provided. Queen Victoria in 1876 made a donation, others followed, and the Prince of Wales came on 10 January 1880 to open a splendid new Institute in Sheet Street – which has already figured frequently in this narrative. The resulting 'Royal Albert Institute' was extended in 1897 when a Grand Bazaar lasting four days was held to pay for it. Princess Christian ran a stall; Queen Victoria gave signed photographs of herself for sale.[7]

Well on into the present century the Albert Institute provided a home for public and cultural occasions, an early and brilliant example of the modern Arts Centres. School plays and, for instance, performances of Gilbert and Sullivan operettas took place there. Mr Pinder has recently drawn attention to the close involvement of St George's Chapel in this century with the Institute,[8] notably when the Minor Canon, Dr E.H. Fellowes, was playing violin solos and editing madrigals for performance there – and many lay clerks were singing at concerts. Schoolchildren as well as adults could buy sheets of tickets to use at choice – one could hear the Boys' School headmaster, Sydney Gammon, lecturing on Westminster Abbey or Father Geoffrey Heald of St Stephen's (who, incidentally, had taught Laurence Olivier how to act as a boy) discoursing on Shakespeare's sonnets. In a front room downstairs was a large (and rather dusty) lending library. On the top floor, a billiard room, with Miss Powell's private preparatory school adjoining. All this largely came to an end with the Second World War. Many of the societies using the Institute had gone; membership declined. In 1950 the Institute was let for educational purposes, and then, in 1966 the Trustees decided to sell the property. With the proceeds a Trust was set up to give help to artistic and cultural activities in the Borough. In

1977 the Institute was rebuilt very elegantly as an office block, and the two original statues of Prince Albert are preserved, the one in a niche over the main entrance and the other in the foyer, commemorating past royal involvement in the life of the Borough and a most active century of artistic life.

References

1 See R.P. Mander, 'The Theatrical History of Windsor', *Curtain Up*, vol iv, no 2, 10 – 11; no 3, 10; no 4, 10 – 11; no 8, 8 – 9; vol vii, no 2, 12 – 13; also O. Hedley, *Queen Charlotte* (1975), 234 – 5, and *Round and about in Windsor* (1950), 89 – 90.
2 One of them, an ex-pupil of Windsor Girls' School is Geraldine McEwan (see the interview with her by Deborah Moggach in *The Times* 7 October 1983).
3 Mervyn Bruxner, *A Hundred years of Music Making, A History of the Windsor and Eton Choral Society 1841 – 1941* (1941), 7 and passim. For the records of the Society see the Minutes books and other documents in BRO.
4 The records of the Windsor and Eton Amateur Orchestral Society 1881 – 1928 are in BRO.
5 BRO holds an extensive series of concert programmes, partly in the series already mentioned, also, eg of St Cecilia's concert at the Swan Inn, 1824.
6 A. Macnaghten, *Windsor in Victorian Times* (1975) provides references to the Mechanics Institutes, eg, 46, 68, 73.
7 ibid, 82 – 3; and BRO.
8 A.T. Pinder, 'St George's Choir and the Royal Albert Institute', RF St G (1977 – 8), 391 – 4.

(vi) The Schools

By the 1960s neither the church nor voluntary cultural groups were as central as they had been a century before. To some extent schools, universities (including most notably the Open University) and colleges of further education have taken over. So far, in narrating the general story of Windsor, formal education does not seem to have played a great part. Admittedly, at Eton College (founded in 1440), there was a school which at the start educated some local children. St George's Chapel choir dating from its still earlier foundation in 1348 contained young trebles, sometimes Windsor boys, who were taught by a schoolmaster – as Neville Wridgway has described in detail[2] – but until the 1700s the main provision for education in the Borough was limited. Firstly, it was a matter of apprenticeship. Basic numeracy and literacy were clearly needed if one were to become a freeman, a trader, and eventually a member of the fraternity. How, say in the 16th century, these were acquired in Windsor there is no evidence. Dames and other private schoolteachers must have been available, as well as the junior clergy, to run one-room schools. The clergy were in any case involved in another way. They had to teach the Catechism, the Ten Commandments and the Creed before children could be presented to the Bishop for confirmation. Some towns went further. Wealthy

The Charity School, St Albans Street in the mid 18th century. The architect was Sir Christopher Wren.

benefactors in the Middle Ages or the 16th century had founded 'grammar schools' which taught not only the three Rs but, as in Shakespeare's case, a little Latin, and perhaps in the later centuries a modicum of Greek – and all this could lead to a University career or to training in one of the London Inns of Court. Windsor was unlucky. Archbishop Laud had helped by leaving £50 a year for binding boys apprentices (and marrying poor girls),[3] but there was no 'King Edward VIth Grammar School', for instance. Quite generally, there was no enthusiasm in the country for education, unless it was specialised, producing priests, barristers or doctors at the end. Many felt that the poor, if educated would come to despise their lot in life and become fractious and rebellious – this was the 'popular' view in the 18th century, according to recent research.

It was, however, in the 18th century that Windsor began to move forward. In 1701 John Porter left money for a school to be established in Priest Street;[4] in 1704 Mary Barker left £360 to be shared by Windsor, Egham, and Yately (Hants) for the teaching of poor children. The history of the *Royal Free Schools* of Windsor, published in 1955, gives the text of the Foundation Deed of the resulting school and of the appeal for subscriptions. The aims of the new school were that the poor children of Windsor:

1. 'May read, write, cast accounts, and be well instructed in the principles of religion'
2. 'be furnished with Bibles and Common Prayer Books'
3. 'be clothed in some sort or other'
4. 'be placed out in the world afterwards'

Queen Anne gave £50, her husband, Prince George, £30, and the Corporation an annual gift of £10. Some Chapter sympathy was represented by £20 from the Dean and Canons, with their Organist rather nobly contributing £1.1.6 on his own account. The Bishop of the diocese gave £5, and Sarah, Duchess of Marlborough, £10. So the school started, perhaps in the church vestry, until in 1726 the handsome classical brick building at the top of Church Lane (now the Masonic headquarters) was ready.

What impact this school had on Windsor for a century is hard to estimate. At the end of the 18th century there were only 57 children in it, who were selected by the trustees, and they still only dealt with the 3 Rs, and with sewing and knitting. But it did better than many charity schools elsewhere at the time. These were in such a poor way that two national religious organisations, the 'British and Foreign School Society', non-sectarian, but in fact mainly nonconformist, in 1810, and the 'National Society for providing education of the poor in the doctrine and discipline of the Established Church', in 1811, came into being.[5] Until 1870 these two societies dominated the educational field in a vigorous but useful competition, covering the land with a network of 'elementary' schools, mainly for children up to 13. Their work was governmentally recognised by the appointment in 1839 of a Committee of the Privy Council on Education and Inspectors were sent out to visit, encourage, chide and report both to the Committee and to Parliament.

In Windsor a National School was set up in 1820.[6] It was in Peascod Street, strongly supported by the Dean and Canons, notably by Canon George Champagné, in whose memory 'Champagné Bibles' are still given by the Chapter. Within 12 months there were 305 pupils. It made sense for the Charity and the National schools to amalgamate. This they did in 1859. The Church Lane building was sold, and the present buildings on Bachelors' Acre, 'The Windsor Royal Free and Industrial Schools', rose on a site acquired in 1861. The school took children between 7 and 16 years, of whom 70 received free clothing as well as education. Additions were made to the building in 1910; and an Infants School in Alexandra Road was an offshoot. Slowly a more substantial type of education developed, with such subjects as algebra, music, history, geology, physiology and esperanto (in 1919), appearing in the syllabus.

In addition, the rival had come to Windsor. The British and Foreign Society, with equal success – though not having the earlier endowments and tradition of a charity school to draw on – was opened in Chariott's Place in 1841, almost next door to the National School, with an outlying building providing a separate Infants School. This school has not yet found its historian, but well into the 20th century it provided an education of similar quality to that of the National School, attended by inter-school games, and by fights on the neighbouring Bachelors' Acre.

A return by the Inspectors showed that towards the end of the 19th century, in 1893,[7] there were places for 538 in the British School; 722 in the National School, with a further 344 in the Infants' school in Alexandra Road. There were 321 in a separate parish school administered by Holy Trinity, and 100 in a church Infants school at Spital – 2,025 in all, by comparison with 57 at the beginning of the century. It should be added, however, that children were often absent. They were sick; they lacked adequate clothing; they were sent to do jobs by their parents; or they simply played truant. So average attendance was only 1,386 out of 2,025.

The churches on the whole were doing well; so the State did little or nothing locally. No School Board was set up for Windsor under the 1870 Education Act, and all Windsor education remained under religious or private auspices at the elementary level until a state school was built in Clarence Road in 1930. The result still noticeable in the 1980s, and a matter of controversy, is that Windsor education includes 'a very strong Church presence'.

But it did not satisfy the more prosperous Windsor residents, and a wide variety of private enterprise shared the educational scene, notably with two relatively prestigious schools in the Alma Road area, Clewer House School and St Mark's School.

St Mark's was much the earlier. It had not started very grandly in 1846;[8] it was 'for the children of the Labouring Class', and it represented the development of an idea of Windsor's notable curate, G.A. Selwyn, twenty years earlier when he had established a small school in 'a washerwoman's cottage, with a small drying ground attached, at the junction of Goswell and Clewer Lane'. 19 boys had attended this school, and although it petered out, the St Mark's foundation of 1846 carried on its main ideas. It was immediately successful. By 1849 a Government inspector described it as 'one of the most successful attempts in elementary education with which I have become acquainted.' It had a lot of good ideas. Thus, 'do not put the boys into an antiquated costume'; give them practical experience of shoeing horses at a smithy, glazing windows in the Royal Gardens, while at the same time encouraging them to have their own books and transferring the

The School Hall and Chapel of the Imperial Service College, Alma Road.

school, *en bloc*, to the sea-side for a summer holiday (in 1861). There were places for about 70 boys, with 20 new boys being admitted each year. Something like a grammar school education was after a time being attempted: 'Cassell's *Latin Grammar* price 8d., being nearly the limit of our classical literature' – but more than the British or National Schools could have managed. The school was driven forward by the enthusiasm of the remarkable Hawtrey family from Eton, notably by the Mathematical Assistant, the Rev Stephen Hawtrey. Daily church services were combined with (for then) 'progressive' education. The Ordnance Map of 1873 shows St Mark's standing exactly on the site of what became the chapel of the later Imperial Service College, surrounded by a large playground just off Alma Road. But it gradually ceased to be a local day school.[9] In 1870 a boarding house was opened and this was later regarded as the foundation of a 'prep. school' in modern jargon. After some uncertain years, in 1894 a small army crammers establishment at Bath (the Hermitage) moved to Windsor and amalgamated with it, contributing a hundred boys. A school intended for the labouring classes had moved up-market; it was run on 'public school lines' and in the following century was to emerge as a notable member of the group of Headmasters' Conference Schools, i.e. as a public school. This was in essence the result of a further amalgamation in 1906 with the United Services College, from Westward Ho on the North Devon coast. This school had been founded in 1874 by a group of retired army officers in order to prepare their boys for Woolwich or Sandhurst. Rudyard Kipling had been a pupil there, 'Twelve bleak houses by the shore, seven summers by the shore' (in fact Kipling spent five years there), but with a gifted headmaster, Cornell Price, an odd and brilliant pacifist running a semi-military establishment. Kipling's *Stalky and Co.* conveys something of the spirit of the school and has assured it permanent fame.[10] But it did not do very well. Effectively it ended in 1903, but sons of its former pupils began coming to Windsor, and in 1906 St Mark's School, rejuvenated by these various amalgamations and increased numbers became the United Services College and, in 1912, the Imperial Service College.

For a time the ISC was an important part of the Windsor scene. Its various houses stretched along Alma Road to the outlying 'Connaught' house in St Leonard's Road, and the intervening quadrilateral was Windsor's small Eton, with masters in caps and gowns and boys in the approved varieties of scholastic and athletic dress rushing from house to classroom, chapel or fields. If the ward of Clewer Without was ecclesiastical, with Sisters of Mercy in wimples and priests in soutanes, that of Clewer Within was public school. Grand gates with heraldic lions were set up in 1926 at the main Alma Road entrance; the Earl of Athlone opened a vast 'King Edward Horse Hall' in 1931 and the school gained a royal charter.[11] But over-ambitious building schemes and stiff competition plus pessimism over the prospects of such schools after the war eventually destroyed the school. Clement Attlee personally had saved it from evacuation in 1939: but in 1942 it merged with Haileybury and in effect ended. Its very much more successful Junior School in Dedworth Manor remained and today serves as a preparatory school for Haileybury. Most of the senior school buildings have been demolished, although one, the 'Rudyard Kipling Memorial Building' served as Municipal Offices for a generation after the last war until the Rank-Hovis complex acquired the greater part of the ISC site in Alma Road from the Borough and established (during 1982 – 3) vast headquarters buildings there. A curious and complicated story, yet for a century and a half a notable contribution to Windsor's educational life.

But while 'St Marks' became more expensive and more exclusive in the latter part of the 19th century a simpler private education was being provided at 'Clewer House School'. The great cedar tree which still stands, most unusually, in one of Windsor's main streets, St Leonard's Road, survives from Clewer House school grounds, and the 'Cottage' in the neighbouring Queen's Road was the school sanatorium. The School probably started in the 1830s as one of the twelve fee-paying schools described by Angus Macnaghten, most of them probably with no more than a teacher each; 'academies', which were still represented in the 1920s

The Rudyard Kipling Memorial Building, Imperial Service College.

by Miss Rule's school in the Acre, and Miss Powell's at the Albert Institute, and each taking some 30 or so children between the ages of about 5 and 8.[12] But Clewer House became something more. It took day boarders, and the diarist Alexander Elliot became one in 1841, staying there for 5 years from 8 to 13.[13] He did not enjoy the experience. 'I never played if I could help it . . . Football I never played, cricket only if I could get to join a small boys' single-wicket touch.' He became the victim of bullies, who on one occasion tried to suspend him from a hat peg. Not an altogether agreeable school, perhaps, though it developed quite ambitiously when in 1883 Mr Nutter Barker came from a Classical and Commercial Academy in Islington where he had been instructing 'Young Gentlemen' in the usual branches of a 'sound and liberal education', including the use of globes, but with 'Position Exercises' as an extra.[14] At Clewer House under his mastership hobbies multiplied – always a good sign – with Natural History and Literary and Scientific Societies, formal Speech Days, and published 'Addresses and Letters'. An address of 16 September 1886 wound up interestingly with the declaration that in education 'Friendship' was the firmest and most enduring thing, and that unless your friend had 'some grave moral defect' friendship should only be given up by mutual consent. But within a decade the school closed, just after St Mark's had expanded in 1894; the competition proved too much.

No grammar school, but a wide range of church and private schools: according to Harrod's *Directory* of 1876 'Few provincial towns of equal extent and population can vie with the royal borough in the number or value of its charitable institutions', (by which it mainly meant the church schools) but emphasising that Windsor also provided academies for young gentlemen, and 'seminaries' and other establishments for young ladies. The verdict is probably a fair one, and again marks the extraordinary contrast between Victorian England and its preceding centuries.

References

1 The foundation charter provided for pupils chosen first from places where Eton College or King's College, Cambridge, had possessions; then from the Counties of Buckingham and Cambridge, and only then from elsewhere. (W. Sterry, *Annals of . . . Eton*, 1898, 52).
2 N. Wridgway, *Choristers of St George's Chapel* (1980).
3 TD, ii, 154.
4 *The Royal Free Schools Windsor, Berkshire* 1955, contains the main source references, with quotations from Inspectors' Reports.
5 On the general history see F. Smith, *History of English Elementary Education 1760 – 1902* (1931), passim.
6 For this para, see n. 4 above.
7 Statistics are derived from the relevant Reports to the Committee of the Privy Council on Education (1859 –).
8 BRO. Rev S. Hawtrey, letter containing an Account of St Mark's School, Windsor (2nd ed. 1859).
9 For the later history of St Mark's see G. Warburton, *Register of St Mark's School, Windsor, 1870 – 90* (1901).
10 Angus Wilson, *The Strange Ride of Rudyard Kipling, his Life and Works* (1979 ed.), 57, 63 – 83, etc. See also M.M. Bendle 'Kipling at Westward Ho' *Country Life* (1983) 1036 – 8.
11 Its notable headmaster, E.G.A. Beckwith compiled *The Imperial Service College 1912 – 1933* (n.d.) which takes the story up to the building of a new boat house in 1933.
12 Macaulay's *Berkshire Directory* (1854) notes that Windsor had 16 schools of which 11 were 'academies', including 2 in Datchet and one in Slough (there has always been a fair amount of educational migration locally).
13 Manuscript diary of Alexander Elliot, with letters, etc, 1817 – 1890, BRO. Elliot would have appreciated G. Painter's aside in *Marcel Proust* i, (1959). 62, where he comments that at the Paris School of Condorcet, 'as in most French schools, violence was as unknown as other organised games; there was no worship of the strong and stupid, and intellectual prowess was respected and encouraged, even by the masters'. This has a sting even for the 1980s.
14 The 'Nutter Barker Papers', 1840 – 1922, BRO, are a fascinating source for the history of this school.

(vii) Sport

When Elliot went to Clewer House school he said he shirked cricket and football. This is a reminder of the part sport played not only in the schools but across the whole range of Windsor Borough and Castle life. There were advantages here for sport: the royal family encouraged horse-racing; Eton College had pioneered both cricket and football; and the Thames made swimming and boating possible. When in the course of the Victorian period organisation came to sport in the country generally it seemed to take a particular hold in Windsor – rising perhaps to a halcyon period in the present century between the two wars.

Cricket led the way.[1] By 1751 Old Etonians were playing the Gentlemen of England, and, historic moment, in 1788 the 'Gentlemen educated at Eton' met the 'Rest of the Schools' on a field in the Portman Estate, London, where a Thomas Lord became ground-bowler to the White Conduit Club, in other words they played at Lord's. Wagers entered greatly into early matches. An unfortunately undated public notice[2] but not much later than 1836, announces in a startling variety of large print: 'CRICKET. A Great Match at Putney For 1,000 Sovereigns between the Eton and Putney Clarence Clubs' with 'Wickets to be pitched at Eight o'Clock'. By 1850 cricket was being played in Windsor Home Park by elevens mainly comprising Eton masters, with Prince Christian as President on one famous occasion enrolling W.E. Grace to join the side. The interest and social respectability of cricket are witnessed by the way in which *The Windsor and Eton Express*, ignoring other sports, except racing, begins in 1879 to comment on cricket matches by Guards' officers, and in 1891 prints full cricket scores weekly. By 1900 as many as 15 matches are described in a single issue, ranging from Eton *v.* Harrow to Windsor Conservatives *v.* Staines Linoleum.[3]

There is no doubt that the Windsor Home Park Cricket Club with its Etonian connections led the way – by the beginning of this century it is being described as 'one of the best in the country' – but other clubs appeared, not only in Windsor schools, but also using a variety of pitches in the Home Park and elsewhere: the Windsor Victoria Club in particular, and the Windsor Alexandra Cricket Club, now the Windsor and Eton Cricket Club. Never a mass sport, cricket yet became at Windsor, as on so many village greens in the second half of Victoria's reign, one of the traditional and even ritual features of national life.

The popular sport, of course, was, as it still is, football. For long this game had not been looked on kindly. Many of its origins were in mediaeval street games where two gangs of unruly youths fought for the possession of the ball.[4] It was even illegal – 'bestlie furie and exstreme violence' was how Sir Thomas Elyot described it in 1531. But changes came in the 1700s with schools such as Eton producing some type of rules – the Eton Wall game was being played from about 1717, but the Eton field game was not standardized until 1897. Everyone knows of William Webb Ellis, who 'ran with the ball' in 1823 at Rugby, starting the distinctly more energetic but episodic game of rugby football. Public schools divided; some played and still play the earlier type of football under the aegis of the Football Association, formed in 1863; most opted for rugby under the Rugby Union set up in 1871. Schoolmasters, as secondary education spread, came to prefer rugby – it was the predominant public school game and it kept 30 boys out of mischief rather than 22. But association football, with its more continuous movement and excitement prevailed with the public at large. By the 1870s there was a Windsor football team, the Windsor Phoenix, which played in the first competitive soccer games in the south and had an annual fixture with the Scots Guards. It seems sometimes to have led to quite as riotous and bloodthirsty scenes as the present generation has known, and it was suppressed. The Windsor and Eton Football Club originated in 1902, being soon greatly helped by royal patronage. King Edward VII granted the club the right to use Stag Meadow (on the edge of the Park at Spital) and for only a peppercorn rent. After the first World War the club had two to three thousand members and was for long entirely local. As the *doyen* of Windsor sport, Leslie Lightfoot recalls on one occasion, when it played Spartan League, 7,000 spectators were present. *The Express* after cold-shouldering the game allowed 'jottings' in 1895 and then in 1900 invited secretaries 'to send reports, writing on one side of the papers only'. The mass entertainment had acquired social respectability.

Rugby came along more quietly. There was a Windsor Rugby club from 1871. It failed, but was revived in 1921 and flourishes, always using Home Park pitches, where it now has a club house and several teams. Together with the Old Windsorians, a separate club originally for the Old Boys of the then Grammar School, rugby now has an established place at last among local sports.[5]

These sports in various ways had royal patronage, at the very least the availability of the Home section of the Royal Parks and the provision of Stag Meadow were of great encouragement in their development. But the sport of kings was a much older one, and an equally important feature in Windsor's life. King Charles II had laid down rules for horse-racing, or more precisely, articles for the running for King's Plates, in order to encourage the breeding of stronger horses, and had arranged and enjoyed the races held on Datchet Mead.[6] But the key date was 11 August 1711 when Queen Anne gave a plate worth 100 guineas for a 'new heat on Ascot Common'. Under George II the course was shifted to its present site on Ascot Heath, and this was assigned to the Crown on condition that the heath be 'kept and continued as a race course for the public use'. There were no stands until the early 1800s, but in 1825 Ascot races acquired a predominant social and ceremonial quality when King George IV rode in the first royal procession to Ascot. For Windsor people, for two centuries since, 'Ascot' has been one of the principal dates in the calendar, if only for the influx of visitors, and it has even attracted the Garter Festival to its ambit, for Garter day now is not St George's day, but always the Monday in Ascot week when the Royal Family and their guests are in residence at the Castle.

Windsor was not content to live in glory reflected from 6 miles away. Present residents in Bolton Crescent may be surprised to know that somewhat informal races were held – probably organised by the Guards Officers quartered nearby – along the Bourne Brook during Victoria's reign. They must have started from what are now the Bolton Road allotments and, crossing the present Bolton Avenue and Osborne Road, finished in the meadow by the brook where it still flows south of Frances Road.[7] But something more organised and effective began in June 1866 when the town held a meeting on Rays Meadow at Clewer (the present Windsor Racecourse) . . . 'the attendance was large; and the business details were managed with Mr Frail's normal excellent business style. The stand, weighing room and telephones are patterns of neatness and usefulness', and the reporter notes that press arrangements were better than at Epsom. Racing continued at Windsor, even through the Second World War – then in order to keep horse-breeding going (when there was even no Ascot). As Berkshire's historian of racing remarks 'The figure of eight course at Windsor is, in its own way, a success story.'[8]

The story of sport at Windsor could be extended almost indefinitely; only two addenda, however, can be included. First, the river has, of course, through centuries given Windsor varied opportunities for recreation, notably for fishing and boating. From 1860 there has been a prestigious Eton Excelsior Club for rowing under the guidance of Eton masters, and the story of the river as recreation has been admirably recorded by two Eton masters, L.S.R. Byrne and E.L. Churchill in their *Eton Book of the River* (1952) – would that other sports had such careful historians.

Second, in summary it must be emphasised that the whole range of popular sport at Windsor, as elsewhere, was the creation of the second half of the 19th century. The cultural life gained some shape in the first half, only to be overtaken by sporting life in the second. By 1900 there were two communal centres for leisure at Windsor: the Royal Albert Institute for the arts, and the Home Park for sport.

References

1 On the general development of the game I have followed H.S. Altham, *A History of Cricket* (1926, new ed. 1962).
2 BRO.
3 cf. WEE, 13 June 1863; 18 July 1891; 21 July 1900; 15 Dec. 1900.
4 For football, see M. Marples, *A History of Football* (1954).
5 Practically nothing has been written about Windsor sports and it has my particular good fortune to be helped by my cousin, Leslie Lightfoot MBE, for 60 years Sports Editor of the *Windsor Express*, in whose phenomenal memory much local history and notably that of sport is stored.

6 On the history of racing locally, see David Boyd, *The Running Horses* (1978).
7 ex inf. L. Lightfoot.
8 Boyd, op.cit.

(viii) Members of Parliament

Looking back over the Victorian era at Windsor as a whole, the picture is one of expansion of building, activities and interests, if also of a woeful lack of attention to the wretched poverty of a quarter or so of its inhabitants. Its Sovereign, the town took to its heart more than any previous ruler; and Queen Victoria is now commemorated by J.E. Boehm's Golden Jubilee (1887) statue at the centre of the town where the four roads, Thames St, High St, Castle Hill, and Peascod Street meet. The Queen very fittingly still presides over the town's continuing life.

Did this new attitude to the monarchy (one that did not develop even for George III) reflect anything about the nature of Windsor politics, often in earlier days Whiggish and anti-court? It was certainly helped by the Queen's total withdrawal from party politics in Windsor. But it also seems to correspond to some sort of political shift. At the beginning of the Queen's reign there were four candidates proposed to represent Windsor in Parliament, and three of these were Liberal. The victors were John Ramsbottom (326 votes) and Robert Gordon (292).[1] Ramsbottom was almost an inevitable winner – former officer in the 16th Dragoons, the representative of Windsor since 1812, and as banker and brewer an important employer of Windsor labour (subsequently a Director of the London and South Western Railway). But the pattern was Liberal. As late as 1865 there were 4 candidates again, and once more 3 were Liberal; the two victors, after an election petition, were both Liberals. Between 1837 and 1865, however, the evolving pattern of national politics was to be seen in local elections. In 1847 there was a successful 'Liberal Conservative', and straight 'Conservatives' began to hold seats from 1841 (Neville) and Lord Charles Wellesley (top of the poll, 1852). When the representation of Windsor was cut to a single member in 1868, the victor was a Liberal, but at the next election in 1870 a Conservative, Robert Richardson-Gardner beat his Liberal opponent by some 400 votes and began a series of Conservative victories that have lasted since over a century. Gardner's association with Windsor is described by Mr Macnaghten,[2] who tells us that Richardson-Gardner was born 'plain Richardson', a builder. He married the daughter of a wealthy Clerkenwell brewer, Henry Gardner, and linked her name with his. He may have come to Windsor as a builder himself, in connection with the construction of the Prince Consort Cottages in the 1850s. Presumably some knowledge of architecture obtained his election as a Fellow of the Society of Antiquaries, and his social standing improved when he raised a

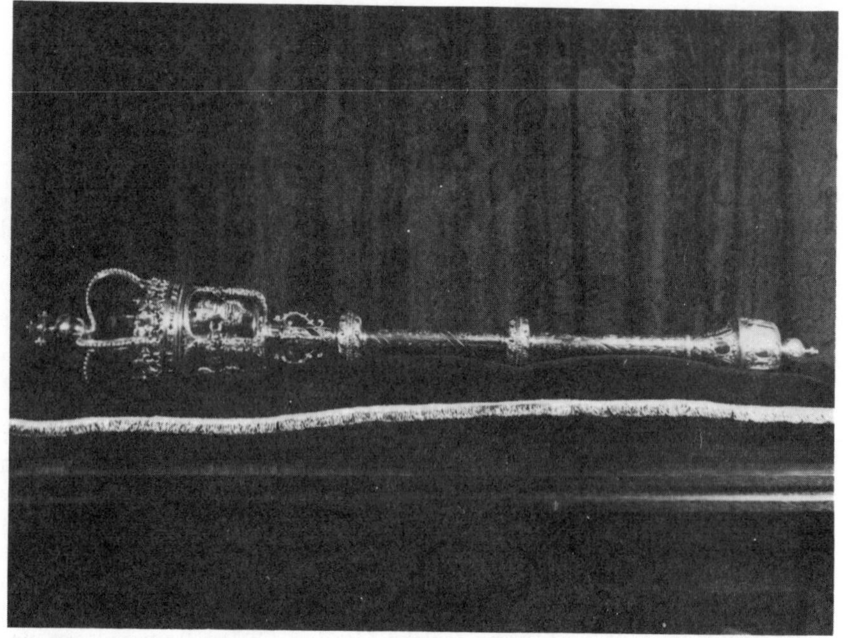

The Mace of the Royal Borough of New Windsor.

corps of militia in Hampshire and became Honorary Colonel of a Rifle division and then Deputy Lieutenant of Tower Hamlets. Unsuccessful candidate for Windsor in 1868, he must have improved his hold on electors by building the Gardner Cottages in Arthur Road in 1870, by leasing 'on very reasonable terms' several hundred of the Goswell slum properties and by, as it was said, a 'liberal distribution of coal and pork pies'. He represented Windsor until 1890, on the whole a popular and munificent local character. His successor, Francis Tress Barry, was equally notable and began rather higher up the social ladder. He was a wealthy dealer in copper who alternated residence between St Leonard's Hill at Windsor (which he rebuilt) and Keiss Castle, Caithness, the two properties together amounting to about 4,500 acres. President of the Royal Albert Institute, he took a genuine interest in local affairs, notably in forwarding the project for cleaning up the riverside area. He so won local esteem that the Liberals allowed him to be unchallenged in 1895, and in 1900 the Borough made him Honorary Freeman. The new riverside road was named after him, Barry Avenue. In 1889 he was made a Baronet. Liberals stood again after this wealthy and active man had died, but he had secured the Windsor constituency pretty firmly for the Conservative interest.[3]

However, among electors there was always opposition, and many inhabitants were not even electors. Windsor in some ways although a small and compact community had no single character, political or social. This may be because there are so many quite separate institutions, ranging from a college of secular canons and, across the river, a college of academic fellows and scholars to quite wealthy groups of traders. It remained in the 19th century rather a federation than a unity. A final glimpse of Victorian Society in Windsor is offered by Arthur Ponsonby in his life of Sir Arthur, his father, the Queen's Private Secretary from 1870 to 1895.[4] The Ponsonbys lived in the Castle, and Arthur remarks that 'the outstanding feature of Windsor, for which it would be difficult to find a parallel elsewhere, was the variety of distinctive elements which were incorporated within its buildings and neighbourhood.' The ancient castle dominated, and 'the frequent presence of the Queen and her Court and the visits of foreign royalty or of Ministers made the humblest residents feel they were in close touch with the centre of all authority. The Dean and Chapter of St George's supplied an ecclesiastical atmosphere resembling that of a cathedral town. A battalion of Guards always stationed in the barracks daily relieved guard on the Castle with their band, and a regiment of Life Guards in another barracks was ready for state occasions. So the military element was prominent.' Further, 'there was the civic life of the Royal Borough and occasionally the excitement of a parliamentary election.' The Ponsonbys enjoyed all this, even if they did not find it wholly satisfactory. It was not self-sufficient; London was less than an hour away. And, a telling point, 'It represented neither real town life nor indeed real country life'. His conclusion: 'The multifarious elements were rather detached and aloof'. This was the Windsor of one of its notable Victorian families. How far has life changed in the present century? Has the mould been broken?

References

1 For these and other election results see Vacher's Parliamentary Companion (1833 –); C.R.P. Dod, *The Parliamentary Companion* (1832 –); J. Whitacker, *Almanac* (1869 –); and P.H. McCalmont, *Parliamentary Poll Book of all Elections 1832 – 1879* (1971). Windsor's MPs are listed by Shelagh Bond in 'A List of Windsor Representatives in Parliament 1302 – 1966' BAJ, vol 62 (1965 – 6), 34 – 44.

2 *Windsor in Victorian Times* op.cit., between 61 and 113.

3 ibid., 69, 86, 95, 99, 115 – 6.

4 A. Ponsonby, *Henry Ponsonby* (1942), 386 – 7.

Windsor Castle in the Twentieth Century

At the conclusion of his great architectural history Sir William St John Hope remarked (in 1913) that it would 'be long before any great expenditure . . . will be needed as regards the buildings in the Upper and Middle Wards'.[1] This precisely worded statement has been proved true during the course of this century. The Upper and Middle Wards remain as Queen Victoria, or, for that matter Sir Jeffrey Wyatville had left them. But Hope was careful in 1913 not to comment on the Lower Ward. He was then working closely with Canon Dalton of St George's Chapel (who was effectively his mentor) and, by 1913 rumours must have been circulating about the safety of the greatest building in the Castle. In point of fact at that very moment St George's was near to collapse. Christopher Wren two centuries before had spoken of St George's Chapel having walls and buttresses 'too nice' which might easily give way to the vault. In spite of repairs carried out by him in the 1680s,[2] by Henry Emlyn and his colleagues in the 1770s, and some patchy works on the nave vault in 1883, concern was still felt as cracks and movements occurred. In 1914 the South Nave buttresses were strengthened, but the First World War diverted attention, and it was therefore not until 1918 that a decisive word was spoken.[3] The chapel architect, Harold Brakespear, told the canons that the 'ruin' of the Chapel was near. The foundations were giving way; the beams did not adequately rest on the exterior walls; the walls themselves were bulging and cracking. The result was ten years' restoration work, difficult and delicate, unique in Windsor's history. Not only were the foundations strengthened, new buttresses added and much new stone inserted, but the entire Choir vault and part of the Nave vault were taken down, examined, repaired and then replaced. After 300 years statues of the King's Beasts were once more placed above the buttresses and battlements – incidentally not only providing heraldic enrichment but also usefully increasing the downward thrust of the walls, and perhaps also emphasising the horizontal lines of the Chapel rather than the pointed Gothic (St George's is in some sense a forerunner of Renaissance building, four-square, rectilinear, almost Classical). In 1930 the restored Chapel was re-opened. Only one feature has since been added, the brilliantly conceived memorial chapel to King George VI, completed in 1969 and the first structure to be added to the Chapel since 1528. With Piper-Reyntiens stained glass, this memorial chapel is a notable addition to the Castle's architecture, and, so far, the only 20th century creation.[4]

Tourists enjoying a visit to Windsor, and the Curfew Tower in Thames Street.

Although in the early 1900s the main Castle apartments remained the Wyatville reconstruction used by Queen Victoria, the Castle's place in the life of the Court changed. In her later years Queen Victoria lived in the

Castle quietly, receiving official visitors and being entertained, between 1881 and 1901, by a series of command performances, but otherwise avoiding state and ceremonial use of the royal apartments. King Edward VII reversed the rôles. He made London, and therefore Buckingham Palace, his headquarters and one of his principal homes. Windsor no longer overshadowed the Palace.[5] But, all the same, to the new King, Windsor was a splendid setting for grand occasions and for the large parties to which the King 'gave a country house intimacy'.[6] Sir John Fortescue stresses the grandeur rather than the intimacy.[7] He describes how on great occasions 'there was hardly room for everyone, even in Windsor Castle, though it has more than 700 doors and 1100 windows. Some of the foreign potentates, generally the least important, made a point of bringing with them an enormous suite, just to give themselves significance. The Castle hummed like a great city'. Sixty men and women worked in the kitchen on such occasions and perhaps 170 guests sat down to dinner. It was then 'a pageant' 'with servants in liveries, scarlet or blue and gold, Yeomen of the Guard in Tudor dress, guests in uniform'. Everything, Fortescue concludes, was done without friction. Edward VII's household was organised and functioned grandly.

And the King was anxious for new developments. The Castle at his instance, received a new form of entertainment when he had a golf course laid out beyond the East Terrace (a beautifully hilarious undertaking in Frederick Ponsonby's description[8]). Above all, the King clearly valued Windsor as a venue for State Visits by many European princely relatives and Heads of State. President Loubet of France visited the Castle ('a spectacular success'[9]) in 1903 as did the King of Portugal, the King of Spain in 1905, Kaiser Wilhelm in 1907, the Russian Tsar in 1909. Osbert Sitwell, a boy at Eton, commented how at such times there was an unrivalled atmosphere of *festa* and gala which even spread down to the school.[10] Queen Alexandra would have liked to have gone further and occupied the State Apartments at Windsor.[11] As Queen, Alexandra began the process, to be continued with still greater determination and skill by Queen Mary, of assembling and identifying valuable works of art in the Castle. 'Our rooms', Alexandra said, 'will be beautiful when furnished with all the splendid, fabulous furniture in the Castle . . . I have been fishing out such treasures from every imaginable room.'[12] This work, developed by Queen Mary and increasingly professionalised, has now made the Upper Ward of the Castle one of the great centres of both decorative and pictorial art in the country, accessible to scholars, and as far as possible, to the public. A sequence of catalogues has been published, and contributions are frequently made to national and international exhibitions from the Castle. For the discerning, the small and changing exhibition of works by Leonardo da Vinci, Holbein and other Old Masters in the Upper Ward alone makes a visit to Windsor rewarding. In the State Apartments are great works by Rubens, Van Dyck, Canaletto and Lawrence, emphasising the importance of the royal collections formed in the first place by Charles I, then by George III, now being given care and attention by the monarchs of the present century.[13]

But, for Queen Alexandra, antiquities, however wonderful, could hardly be expected to come first. The Queen's initial triumph at Windsor was in 1903, when for the first time for 60 years a State Ball of unusual magnificence was held in the royal apartments, followed by a Garden Party – better than Buckingham Palace even King Edward admitted.[14] These parties were not all ceremonial; Arthur Benson found royal parties rather full of ragging, as, for example, when the King of Portugal in 1903 took to cramming handfulls of snow down the necks of his staff and hurling huge snowballs at them – they in return making up snowballs of the size of marbles and throwing them gingerly back, taking care to miss.[15]

King George V, after his accession in 1910, maintained, with less ragging, this use of the Castle. Special trains continued to bring ambassadors and royalty to Windsor, especially at seasons when covers could be arranged in the Great Park. The area near Bishopsgate was favoured since 'owing to the undulating nature of the ground, the birds are very tall and come fast and high'. At one of these parties, however, the German Ambassador, who 'hated shooting' very sensibly retired to enjoy the treasures of the Royal Library. During the First World War, what parties there were lacked alcohol, to the amazement of Lord Rosebery, who did not recognise the names of any of the soft drinks offered to him (reluctantly he chose ginger ale, which gave him a bad attack of hiccups).[16] After the war George V continued to give parties, filling the Upper Ward to capacity. Windsor meant much to him, and it is not surprising that when during the First World War he had to seek a new non-German name for his family, he chose that of Windsor, and the dynasty remained until recently that of the House of Windsor.[17]

Some sort of shift back from Buckingham Palace to Windsor became inevitable when the Second World War broke out in 1939. King George VI and Queen Elizabeth insisted on spending their working days so far as possible in London. But the Palace was twice bombed in 1940 and it was clearly safer not only for them during periods of bombing to sleep each night in the Castle, but also to arrange for the Princesses Elizabeth and Margaret to make Windsor their permanent home.[18] Thus the present Queen is one of the very few monarchs – Edward III and Edward VI are of their number – to have been brought up at Windsor. The Princesses joined with the children at the Park School in the production of plays. Pantomimes were annual events, and, as the Princesses grew older, small dances were arranged for them at Windsor. Whenever possible King

George VI went riding with them in the Park, having tea with them at the small country house in the Park known as Royal Lodge (near the Bishopsgate entrance).[19] This lodge had been given to King George VI when he was Duke of York, by his father, and since 1931 had served as a country home for the family. The Duke had immediately begun to develop the neighbouring gardens, now known as the Savill Gardens, after his Deputy Ranger, Sir Eric Savill. Princess Elizabeth, when receiving the Honorary Freedom of the Royal Borough in 1947, recalled that 'this town, whose name my family bears, is very dear to me. Indeed, I regard it as home in a way no other place can be'. And so, during her reign since 1952 there has been not only full 'official residence' at Christmas and Easter, and in Ascot week, but very frequent, sometimes daily, informal use by the Queen and Prince Philip of the private apartments. Windsor people are well accustomed to a quick glance when they go into town ('up street' in local parlance) to see which flag is flying over the Round Tower. When it is not the Union Jack but the Royal Standard they know that the Sovereign is in the Castle. State visits and what might be called Edward VII's Windsor routine continue, but with new developments, such as the polo matches on Smith's Lawn in the Park, in which Prince Philip and Prince Charles participate, as they also have in the annual Horse Shows in the Home Park.

The life and significance of the Castle have certainly been quickened during recent decades. The same can be said about St George's Chapel. Although by foundation a relatively restricted group of clergy and laity, the Chapel has always been open to the public, whether by its organisation of pilgrimages and by its daily services, or simply as a tourist attraction. Any possible isolation was further diminished by two new organisations in this century which between them have considerably extended the influence of the chapel. In 1931, immediately after the completion of the structural restoration, Dean Albert Baillie[20] formed a society of 'Friends of St George's', to help towards the preservation of the Chapel and its furnishings. This Society has flourished, gaining some thousands of members and contributing the widest possible support to the Chapel, ranging from the purchase of a splendid mediaeval statue of the Madonna and Child to the complete rebuilding of the Western Steps. Equally importantly, it has involved large numbers of local residents in the day to day life of the Chapel. Friends act as stewards, help organise concerts, or do the hundred and one jobs that made the Chapel's celebration of a Quincentenary in 1975 so notable a success.[21] The gap between Castle and borough suggested by Ponsonby has in this way been greatly diminished.

Then, Baillie's successor but one as Dean, Robin Woods, presided in 1966 over the establishment of a conference centre in the heart of the Chapel's precincts. Minor Canons' residences (over-large) became a hostel (often over-crowded now); a one-time Canon's home was converted for a

Prince Charles at a meeting of the British Equestrian Association in 1982.

Warden's headquarters. The Chapter Library doubled as a discussion centre. Fifty groups on average have since met in 'St George's House', as it is called, each year. A third are of clergy who examine the role of the Church in modern society; the rest are for those in industry, government and other institutions of society in order to consider specific issues. One of the most important movements towards church unity, the report of the Anglican-Roman Catholic Commission, issued in 1982, just before the Pope's visit, resulted from seven groups of decisions, three of which were agreed by members at meetings in St George's House. The Castle thus now welcomes a continuous stream of trade union members, business executives, Members of Parliament, broadcasting officials, and many others as well as clergy to live within it, for a week, a week-end or perhaps a month. The conference centre links the Castle and Chapel in an entirely original way with various streams of national and international life.

A more traditional and abiding aspect of the life of the Chapel is its music. A strong Choir school supports Lay Clerks and Organist in making the St George's Choir one of distinction, able to range from mediaeval polyphony to Benjamin Britten and Philip Cannon. Not least important was the work of a single man, Dr Edmund Fellowes, Minor Canon from

1900 to his death in 1951. Fellowes sang the services devotedly and for a time was Master of the Choristers, but his real work was done in libraries and universities, producing texts of what was then all but unknown music, both religious and secular. Today in the 1980s it is a familiar and vital part of the world's musical repertory. His editions of William Byrd's music and of other Tudor composers, together with his history of *English Cathedral Music*, are classics. In Fellowes, Windsor nurtured one of the great musicologists of the century, and one of the two or three most gifted scholars of its history.[22]

Finally, St George's, having gained two new types of impetus, from the Society of the Friends and the Conference centre, has also developed a not unimportant additional form of creative activity in the field of publication and scholarship. When, in 1936, S.L. Ollard was appointed to a canonry and Sir Owen Morshead presided in the Upper Ward over the Royal Library, the Chapter initiated a series of publications known rather forbiddingly as 'Monographs' in order to make more generally accessible the great stores of documents preserved in the Aerary (i.e. Treasury). These documents date from the 12th century and range from papal bulls and royal charters to everyday matters such as the cost of repairing windows broken by pet monkeys and the everyday life of the community. Canon Dalton had made a catalogue of the main contents of the Aerary (but had failed to publish it). Morshead and Ollard between them started a series which now not only includes Dalton's Catalogue, but a wide range of subject lives of the Canons, Military Knights and Minor Canons to the Monuments of the Chapel, and, shortly, its Stained Glass. St George's as a result is now probably the best documented church in the country. A professional archivist took charge of the Aerary in 1947, and his successor is now in regular attendance, providing a search room for members of the public and dealing with a continuing stream of correspondence.

The 20th century has in many ways brought the Chapel closer to church, nation and the world at large. Yet, perhaps a final comment from an Eton boy takes us back to the underlying message of the Chapel. John Lehmann in his autobiography, *The Whispering Gallery*, recalls how he once represented Eton College in placing a sheaf of lilies on the Founder, Henry VI's, tomb in the Chapel. This 'gave us a strange feeling of escaping from the enclosing barriers of school life into a timeless symbol, a moment in the sky.'[23]

References

1 Hope, 369.

2 ibid., 386 – 8.

3 The basic authority for the repair of St George's is the bound set of *Brakespear's Reports* 1918 – 1930 (privately printed for the Chapel) which include, doubtless with Dalton's help, historical retrospective comments.

4 RF St G (1969), 421 – 5.

5 S. Lee, *King Edward VII*, ii (1927), 19, 67, etc.

6 ibid., 70.

7 J.W. Fortescue, *Author and Curator* (1933), 97.

8 F. Ponsonby, *Recollections of Three Reigns* (1951), 135 – 6.

9 Lee, op.cit., ii, 245.

10 O. Sitwell, *The Scarlet Tree* (1946), 272. For the actual visits see eg. *Journals and Letters of Viscount Esher* (1903 – 10), 31, 53, 254, 318 etc.

11 G. Battiscombe, *Queen Alexandra* (1969), 219.

12 ibid.

13 See J.H. Plumb and Huw Wheldon, *Royal Heritage* (1977), and, same authors, *Royal Heritage, The Reign of Elizabeth II* (1981).

14 Battiscombe, op.cit., 252; Lord Ormathwaite, *When I was at Court* (1937), 106.

15 David Newsome, *On the Edge of Paradise* (1980), 103.

16 Ormathwaite, op.cit., 197, 221.

17 H. Nicholson, *King George V* (1967 ed.), 405 – 6. His MS speech announcing this to the Mayor and people of Windsor is in BRO. The dynasty since 1960 has been 'Mountbatten – Windsor'.

18 J.W. Wheeler-Bennet, *King George VI* (1958), 468, 740 – 1.

19 ibid.

20 Dean Baillie's autobiography, *My First Eighty Years* (1951) is an informative and engaging book.

21 See annual RF St G, and, in particular, *The St George's Chapel Quincentenary Handbook* (1975) with the important article by J.R. Lande, A.K.B. Evans, and Peter Kidson.

22 See E.H. Fellowes, *Memoirs of an Amateur Musician* (1946); likewise for this period of the Chapel history, A.C. Deane, *Time Remembered* (1945).

23 J. Lehmann, *The Whispering Gallery* (1955), 99 – 100.

The Borough in the Twentieth Century

(i) At the turn of the century

The mediaeval town, as we have seen, remained largely unchanged in its built-up area from 1500 to 1800. Sudden expansion came with both Regency villas and Victorian slums until about 1840. Then although a number of separate villas were built, general urban expansion, rather oddly, slowed down. The second great growth period was between 1880 and 1914, a period, at least on superficial evidence, of marked prosperity for Windsor, a period with an increasing number of quite well-to-do middle class, and a small but important group of members of the nobility and wealthy gentry, who wished, perhaps, to have a second home for the Ascot season and for other periods of the royal residence.

Angus Macnaghten in his *Victorian Windsor* provides chapter and verse for much of this development. Here only a general survey, going well into the Edwardian period, is possible.[1]

Firstly there are the houses, nearly all still surviving, for the upper working and lower middle classes, for shop assistants, lawyers clerks, builder's workmen, Castle servants, and for those working in Windsor's four large and prosperous breweries.[2] The main building area was south of Victoria Street, well away from both the gentry in Clarence Crescent, and the slums beyond, lining a series of new roads: Alexandra Road (1875), Albany Road (1895), Temple Road (1891), Springfield Road (1898), Bolton Road (1899), Victor Road (1898), Bourne Avenue (1898), and the outer part of St Leonard's Road, with individual detached houses, from 1880 onwards. As late Victorian domestic architecture these housing developments of private enterprise, without benefit of architect, have interesting features. There is a progressive abandonment of gothic pointed arches and window frames, in preference for more classical features, such as semi-circular arches, square headed windows, even capitals and pilasters. Although this block of roads in Windsor superficially all look alike, there is a wide variety of quite expensive ornament and decoration: zig-zag brickwork, rosette and other patterned brick panels, stained-glass windows for the front doors, bow windows of varied design. Even in a long terrace each house calls itself a 'villa', though there were often groups of two or more with names on a date label recalling a birthplace, honeymoon or child's name.

Houses in Alexandra Road built about 1875.

Some hundreds of houses were built in the post-1880 period; but there are two particularly interesting groups. The early Victorian expansion culminated in the building of Holy Trinity Church, the later development began with a church, the large and very typical mid-Victorian gothic church of All Saints, built in 1863. This church was the work of Sir Arthur Blomfield, the architect of Selwyn College, Cambridge (an interesting link with Windsor's former curate), the Royal College of Music, London, and many churches. One of his early pupils was the future poet and novelist, Thomas Hardy, and Hardy is reputed to have been the draughtsman of All Saints. A large airy brick building, All Saints has a wonderful sense of space and has proved over a century a well-loved local religious centre.

Then, a quarter of a mile away from All Saints, the new development produced a splendid block of shops in a non-gothic but still rich Victorian style, once known as the Onslow Buildings, spanning the distance from Albany to Temple Road along St Leonard's Road. Nearly all retain their Victorian shop-fronts (a mercy), and also, unaltered upper structures, which form a carefully designed unit, elegantly decorated. Two companion pieces appear at the further ends of both Temple and Albany Roads, where the corner houses adjoining Alexandra Road break away from the terrace-villa plan and provide architect-built houses with marked Doulton influence, good swag decoration and moulded terracotta tiles – this Doulton influence is quite widely noticeable in Windsor's late-Victorian housing. All this is solidly built, with minimal back-gardens, and capable of the adaptation it has generally received in the post-1946 period. The terrace effect and overall unity are now somewhat spoilt by sporadic whitewashing and new double glazing, but all in all these houses still form a vital part of Windsor's housing stock.

Moving away from the St Leonard's Road – All Saints area towards the Long Walk and Park, something quite different is happening. The gentry's houses in Osborne Road, and still more, in King's Road or Bolton Avenue are grander. They were in fact conceived as small country houses standing in several acres of ground, with servants' cottages and stables scattered around. One example is the house known as 'Queen's Acre', or, to its inhabitants, 'Qu'Acre' on the corner of Bolton Road and King's Road. This fine redbrick house, in an eclectic Renaissance style, was the home of Howard Sturgis, author of *Belchamber*, and an English base for his two American friends, Henry James and Edith Wharton. Arthur Benson was also one of this circle, and he has described in *Memories and Friends* (1924) how Sturgis had made the garden beautiful 'with sheltered walks and rose-trellises and a blue-paved fountain-basin.' The house he enlarged, giving it a big long library and a spacious verandah. 'A most liveable house', Benson concludes.[3]

Its neighbour, across Bolton Road and nearer to the Long Walk, is no less notable. 'Queensmead' is now a convent-school, but for long it was the home of Lord and Lady Edward Spencer-Churchill. This was built in 1880, a long seven-bayed brick building of three storeys, with large Elizabethan type glazed windows and a round-headed arched portico, topped by decorative scroll brickwork and, above it, a lead dome with its weather-vane. There was a stable block, and there still is an endearing smaller road-side lodge, with an armorial brick device. Even in 1880 all trace of gothic had gone; the era of 'Jacobethan' had come, and very impressive it still is, even after recent scholastic attachments to it. A few hundred yards away, at the angle between Osborne Road and Bolton Avenue stood the mock-Tudor half-timbered country house, complete with stables and servants' quarters, which the then Lord Braye called 'his villa' and to which he retired when the care of his hereditary home at Stanford Hall, Northants, proved too much for him.[4]

In 1903, among Windsor's noble residents were not only the Spencer-Churchills at Queensmead, but also, as their neighbours, in King's Road, the Countess of Arran, and Baron Campbell von Laurence, with Sir Charles Cameron, bart., the Dowager Lady Dimsdale, the Hon. Mrs Irby, the Earl Mount-Cashell and the Marquess of Normanby all round the corner in Osborne Road, and Lady St Leonards as a neighbour of Lord

Braye's in Bolton Avenue. The reign of Edward VII saw the apogee of this aristocratic growth of Windsor between Osborne Road and the Great Park. Today some of the houses are gone; most of the rest are flats; and few if any members of ennobled families live in the Borough.

References

1 For the urban expansion see the various editions of the Ordnance Survey maps, and for the streets, a Windsor Local History Publication *The Streets of Windsor* (1980) by Judith Hunter and others.

2 Brewing had always been a staple industry for the whole county, and particularly for Windsor. Norden's Survey shows casks by the Dean and Canon's stables; in the 19th century brewing came to be divided between John Canning's Royal Brewery; John Lovibond and Co.; Burge and Co.; and Neville Reid and Co. (VCH, i, 404 – 11).

3 Benson, op.cit., 279 – 81. There is a marvellous account of Henry James's visit to Qu'Acre in Edith Wharton, *A Backward Glance* (1934), 239 – 43.

4 Lord Braye, *Fewness of My Days* (1927), 299.

(ii) The Edwardian age

The new century in Windsor saw very much more than an increase in its social standing. It witnessed a growth in social consciousness. Three new institutions in particular symbolised this: a new Police Station; the foundation of the County Boys' School; and the construction of the King Edward VII Hospital.

Windsor council, so far, had not been particularly inclined to undertake new initiatives, but encouraged and goaded by a small group of members including Councillor Stoneham, the solicitor F.T. Ryland (who was radical enough to wish to abolish aldermen), and the stationer Councillor Luff, something like the first municipal centre, albeit mainly a police station, was created. The Guildhall, even as it had been extended in 1828, provided few facilities except for Council meetings. There were no offices for officials – Windsor was mainly administered from the office of whichever solicitor acted as Town Clerk. The prison in Sheet Street was small and derelict. So when in 1904 plans were drawn up for a new Police and Fire Station there was a good deal of support. The Mayor, Sir William Shipley, laid a foundation stone in 1905 and by 1906 the growing structure was being described as the 'Municipal Buildings'. It was to house all Borough officials, and Councillors were busy voting on linoleum, furniture, blinds and even 'a cupboard'.[1] In 1907 the new 17 bay building was opened. It stood, as it still in part does, in St Leonard's Road on what had been the Keppel estate. It was made up of a handsome block of red brick and stone far from Victorian gothic – informal elements of early Renaissance character such as rusticated corner pillars combine with a certain amount of Baroque swagger to produce Windsor's only really handsome 20th century building, and certainly one characteristic of the Edwardian epoch, even slightly suggesting in its sturdy appearance the monarch himself.

As it turned out, of all the municipal competitors for the building, the police got the lion's share. This happened at a time when the Borough was fighting the County (successfully) to maintain its own independent police force. The Chief Constable gained a fine residence in the southernmost bay, then came the police offices, and on the other side of the main entrance and a lavish staircase, the Magistrates' Court and retiring room. The end two bays were handed over to the energetic and able Volunteer Fire Brigade, which had been founded in 1867. Prisons and the fire exercise yard lay behind. Borough officials gained nothing, and efforts to make a large room in the basement a Borough Office immediately resulted in a drill-hall being installed there although the Treasurer subsequently gained some desks in the building. But civic consciousness had shown a new spirit of enterprise.

So far as education was concerned, local authorities continued to leave matters to the churches and to private enterprise, until the County moved in 1906 to establish a County School for Boys[2] in Windsor. The Education Committee of the County purchased 'Church House' next to Holy Trinity Church, with grounds stretching down the side of Claremont Road, from the Hawtrey Trustees for £3,900. This was a make-do affair. Church House was a not very good mid-Victorian gothic building, but large enough to take the 40 boys who constituted the first classes, in September 1908. A new block of laboratories with a school hall over provided basic accommodation, to be augmented in 1921 by two temporary huts which remained in use until the school left the site in 1938 for its present home in Maidenhead Road.

The Boys' County School at its first speech day was exhorted to be 'a great school, not only in Berkshire, but in England' and under notable Headmasters, George Wade, the bearded and indomitable founder, the scholarly and dignified S.R. Gibson and the brilliantly imaginative and inspiring Sidney Gammon, the 'W.C.B.S.' acquired, certainly by 1929, a very high academic reputation. A fee-charging school, until the 1944 Act came into operation, it yet admitted many boys from the church elementary schools on 'free places', and also received 'county scholars' who had been successful in county competitive examinations. Wade started it on a 'public school' system, with houses, prefects, and so on. But unlike the necessarily isolated and sometimes introverted boarding schools, the County Boys School became very much part of its local community. The Borough appointed representative governors and within four years was recording the success attained by its pupils and seeking an increase in scholarship or free places. Speech days and school plays took place in the Royal Albert Institute; practice in games led to the formation of Old Windsorian teams for old boys and to a strengthening of local athletic and sporting clubs.

So great an impact did the school have on local opinion that in May 1919 the Borough council urged the County Council to establish a similar school for girls – threatening to put a scheme of its own to the Board of Education if the County did not show more initiative.[3] Windsor councillors said there was a strong demand for a girls' secondary school, to secure free places from the elementary schools, to train pupil-teachers, and to offer non-denominational education. The county acquiesced, and in September 1920 the County School for Girls opened. Like the boys, the girls had to accept unsuitable Victorian accommodation (in Osborne Road), but again, this did not prevent notable success. Margaret Curtis, the outstanding inter-war head, combined in herself many of the virtues of the three successive boys' headmasters. She entered vigorously into local life and on retirement became Honorary Secretary of the Friends of St George's Chapel. The two schools had got off to a good start. In the 1970s they were re-organised with notable success as upper comprehensive schools, but at the moment of writing falling rolls (resulting from falling birthrates) are possibly leading to yet more re-organisation – but now in terms of a school roll not of 40 but of 600 or 700.

The third new Edwardian innovation was a Hospital. Agitation had been mounting in the Borough as pressure on the old Victoria Street Dispensary of 1834, with its annexed Infirmary of 1857, became almost intolerable. In 1903 there were 328 in-patients, in 1907, 507 (in the same space), with, in the latter year, some 3000 out-patients.[4] Extension of the buildings on Bachelors' Acre was out of the question. As so often, Prince Christian solved the problem, obtaining permission for 3 acres of Crown land, opposite to the Combermere Barracks, for use as a new site, and then presiding over the whole business of subscriptions and designs until in 1908 King Edward VII spread cement on the foundation stone 'in workmanlike manner derived from experience in laying many commemorative and foundation stones', as the reporter commented. A.W. West was the architect – rather oddly he was the Treasurer of St George's Hospital, London, but his building was innovatory. Windsor Council waived its by-law that all structures should be of brick or stone, and West built on an American framework principle. Steel frames were filled with Frazzi blocks of clay, rough cast on the outside and plastered on the inside. A brick hospital would have cost £50,000; this cost £25,000.

By June 1909 a children's ward, two operating rooms and a chapel were in use. The operating rooms had been equipped with funds raised by a Second Life Guards Band concert. On the anniversary of the laying of the foundation stone an Open Day attracted a thousand visitors 'mostly of the poorer classes' and, with the help of Prince and Princess Christian the new foundation was commemorated by the erection of a statue in bronze to

King Edward in the forecourt.[5] This was designed by the Countess Feodora Gleichen, grand-daughter of Queen Victoria's half-sister, but a professional, competing anonymously. Her statue is a notable Renaissance type piece, high on a stone pedestal, with four Michelangelesque fullsize draped female figures at the corners, representing 'Intuitus, Felicitas, Sapientia, Humanitas', the virtues of the good nurse, tact, geniality, wisdom and humanity. The Countess had caught very well the new 20th century feeling for the Renaissance and Classical traditions. Gothic is over (for the time being). The Hospital itself has since received many additions and is the principal of its type in east Berkshire, still known as 'King Edward's'.

To these three public institutions should be added one of the best public amenities also still enjoyed by Windsor – the Alexandra Gardens along the riverside. Planning for these was a Victorian achievement (in 1893); land was purchased in 1895. Plantations were in hand in 1905. A bandstand in the centre,[6] lawns, flower-beds, tennis courts, and, a little further on, swimming baths, completed an amenity especially valuable to the slum-dwellers who lived only the other side of a railway line which marks the boundary of the gardens. Ballast heaps had to be removed and private meadows bought. A century later the Alexandra Gardens remain one of the most agreeable features of the town, linking urban and riverside life.

Other initiatives appeared in the pre-war period, but one of these, the most important, failed. This was a proposal to accept a Carnegie grant in order to establish a public library, and, in 1912, the Vicar of Windsor's suggestion that a free library should be established met an equally frosty reception.[7] However, it began to dawn on the town that much of its property was supremely unattractive and just before the war, after hesitation, the council agreed to consider the 'possibility of improving the town to make it more attractive as a place of residence.'[8] The war intervened, but, as we shall see, this bore fruit ultimately in the 1920s and finally eradicated the 'Two Nations' appearance of Windsor, which in Victoria's reign had brought down governmental critcism on the town and its council.

A steadily improving town made it a still more attractive focus for the state visits beloved by King Edward. The Borough happily produced quite lavish street displays to welcome visiting sovereigns – of Italy in 1903, of Spain in 1905, and of Greece in 1906. But either nationalist feelings or finance led to debate in 1907. Should the German Emperor's visit be paid for by subscriptions after a public meeting, or should the ratepayer finance it? By 18 votes to 3 the Council decided in favour of the rates, and the usual 'Decoration Committee' was set up,[9] as it was also for the King of Portugal in 1907. Windsor felt it was part of the international scene, and was prepared to pay for it. There was also the very real affection for the visiting monarchs' host, King Edward. On his death the Council, in an address to the new King, George V, referred to a reign which had been 'characterized by his desire to maintain the peace of the world.' George V, in a warmly responsive mood, told the Windsor burgesses that he and they 'have been neighbours already for many years and we shall now be drawn together in that still closer . . . which has for centuries united your Ancient and Royal Borough to the Sovereigns of this Realm.'[10]

Many of the Edwardian developments, even if arising from initial intervention from radical councillors, became the close concern of a councillor, essentially conservative but typical of the very much more interventionist and socially conscious city fathers of the twentieth century. Sir William Shipley laid the foundation stone of the Municipal Buildings, housing the Police Station and Fire Station obtained finance for the new Hospital, supported, and indeed for a time owned, the Theatre Royal, being responsible for the construction of the present theatre building in Thames Street. Alderman, and then Mayor of the Borough for three successive years, he was also a County Councillor and Windsor's representative on the Thames Conservancy Board. He had wealth – he owned Burges' Brewery – but as the Vicar of Windsor said at his death,[12] Shipley was 'not like many rich men who having made their money in a place, went and spent it elsewhere'; Shipley's radical opponent, Councillor Luff, called him 'a real man'.

There were others of similar calibre, one group forming a unique family succession, that of the Dyson family; Thomas Dyson came in the 1860s to sing as a Lay Clerk of St George's from Yorkshire and successfully stood for election as Councillor in 1883 (there were raised eybrows at St George's). Becoming Alderman in 1894 he continued until 1903, and was at the receiving end of the government enquiry we have described into, and disapproval of, Windsor's sanitation. The Riverside Promenade, intended to keep back the frequent Thames flooding was one of the more fortunate results of the encounter, and today its chief and only monument is the marble 'Dyson Memorial Fountain' of 1903. In that year his son, Charles Frederick Dyson, was elected Councillor, becoming Alderman in 1926 and serving three times as Mayor, being knighted in 1911. He continued the two adjacent shops his father Thomas had owned in Thames Street, one a jewellers, still there under family control, and the next door pianoforte warehouse (established by 1869). Sir Frederick died in 1934, and the family civic activity lapsed until his nephew, Cyril Douglas Dyson became Councillor in 1943 and Alderman in 1951, like his uncle serving as Mayor, being knighted, and gaining wide respect as a wise and hard-working administrator. He left the council in 1961, whilst continuing to manage, as now his son does, Dyson's Jewellers Shop in Thames Street.

The 80 years of Dyson service in some sense are eclipsed by the remarkable record of Sir William Carter,[13] a Marlow elementary schoolboy, then painter, decorator and gardener, before settling as a Prudential Assurance Agent at Windsor, aged 31 in 1879. Councillor in 1902, Alderman in 1922, and Mayor for 13 years in all – this is unequalled in Borough history from the earliest records of the Mayorality in the fourteenth century (maximum continuity in office had been for three or four years). Like Shipley, Carter served the Hospital and countless local societies. Unlike Shipley he was not a rich man, but one extremely generous to those who needed, for instance, an interest-free loan to buy a house. A man with splendid white moustaches, his character seems to have attracted and amused the then Prince of Wales. The Prince at a Venison Dinner in 1928, paid his tribute, as High Steward, to Carter for 'having steered Windsor safely through the war, with the same skill and energy with which he still steers his own bicycle up High Street' (at the age of 70). Carter was reputed then to have challenged the Prince to a bicycle race up the hill of Thames Street. The lives of Shipley, Dyson and Carter all suggested the clear and highly personal form of local leadership Windsor enjoyed right up to the dissolution of the Borough in 1974.

References

1 BRO.
2 On the Boys' School, see *The History of Windsor County Boys School 1905 – 1929* (1929), and *Windsorian Magazine* (February 1958).
3 BRO.
4 For a general account of the new hospital see WEE, 22 June 1908.
5 WEE.
6 The band of the Royal Horse Guards was authorised to play in the Alexandra Gardens on Wednesdays from 3 to 5 pm., BRO.
7 BRO.
8 ibid.
9 BRO.
10 ibid.
11 BRO.
12 WEE, 13 Oct. 1922.
13 See the WEE, 9 Nov. 1932 for an account of Carter's career. Various Carter papers are preserved in BRO, (which includes the MS speech of King George V in 1918 announcing his taking the Dynastic title of 'Windsor').

(iii) The First World War

The Prince of Wales' reference to Carter's leadership in the War of 1914 typified an even closer relationship with the royal and national authorities that resulted from that War. Hostilities had been declared on 4 August 1914. All too soon the *Windsor Express* was printing lists of men killed in action, together with vivid and dramatic letters written from the front to relatives. The Berkshire Regiment figured much in these. 'The gallant

The Life Guards departing for the Front on August 15th 1914, passing the Police Station and Fire Station in St Leonards Road.

Berkshires were again in action against the Turks' (in 1915); 'the gallant little Berks, who seem to bear a charmed existence, lost only one horse, two others being slightly wounded' – with other letters much more tragic.[1] Women took the place of men in Windsor banks, the post office, railway stations, and as chauffeurs. Residents raised money by flag days, and in 1915 were called to join in a National Thrift Campaign: 'choose cheaper nutrition, eat less meat, and invest every penny so saved in the War Loan'. Emphatic support was given to the Government, even by the radical Councillor Stoneham, who declared 'it was not possible for anyone to doubt that this was a righteous war'. At a time when the political direction of the war seemed to need support, the Council resolved, on 10 November 1915, that it had 'Entire confidence in the present Coalition Government, and its determination to give the government its whole-hearted support in carrying the war to a successful issue'.[2] The following year, Admiral Jellicoe was congratulated on 'the splendid services rendered by the Fleet' and 'the magnificent result of the recent North Sea Battle'.[3] As sons of prominent burgesses were killed, the Council commemorated their services; but the final toll on life is set out in the panels of the War Memorial in High Street, constructed beneath the Parish Church graveyard. These panels contain just over 300 names. The memorial has at its head a carved crucifix, a symbol thus restored to High Street three centuries after Bishop

Goodman's was banished. The loss of life for Windsor people in the First World War recorded here was nearly three times that suffered in the Second World War,[4] and clearly the greatest in any war in our history.

The King and Queen were often at Windsor during the war. Queen Mary in April 1917, quite unusually, drove ceremonially through the town,[5] and when, a month later, it was whispered (though not in Windsor) that the King must be pro-German, since he and his family had German names, it is recorded by Sir Harold Nicolson that the King 'started and grew pale', then seeking advice on what name, indubitably English, could be adopted. He was offered names such as 'Tudor-Stewart', 'D'Este' and 'Fitzroy'. Then Lord Stamfordham proposed the name of Windsor and this was adopted. Lord Rosebery afterwards congratulated Stamfordham on the rare honour of having 'christened a dynasty'.[6] The crucial factor seems to have been that Edward III, born in the Castle and christened there, had been known, as we have seen, as Edward of Windsor, and Edward III, after all, had won great battles and had founded the Order of the Garter. The Privy Council approved the new name on 17 July 1917,[7] and in September, to commemorate the event, George V presented State Portraits to the Corporation of himself and Queen Mary (to which the Queen added a portrait of Queen Alexandra when she noticed that one was lacking in a series that went back to Queen Elizabeth I).[8] At the presentation of the portraits in the Castle on 24 April 1918 the King remarked that 'My ancestors have been connected with Windsor Castle for many centuries, but curiously enough my family has never had a name'.[9] He had in fact been told by a herald that although everyone assumed the family name was German it was not certain whether this name was Guelph, Wipper or Wettin. Perhaps all this was relatively trivial in the midst of a war, but it certainly bound the monarchy explicitly to the Borough more clearly than had ever been the case before.

The war drew to its close. Soldiers camped in the Park made some use of accommodation in the Police Station and Guildhall. A communal kitchen[10] was serving some 5,000 portions of food and 80 gallons of soup a week to the poor. When Armistice Day came on 11 November 1918 the *Express* lamented the death of 'a million Britishers', and the sorrow throughout the country was almost overwhelming. The paper rejoiced that the 'military dominance of Prussia is now finally destroyed' and 'a braggart King, styled All Highest, cast out by his deluded people'. Windsor celebrated with a parade and a torchlight procession, but there was no 'mafficking', except that the County Boys burned an effigy of the Kaiser on a bonfire.[11] The Council formally addressed the King 'on the great victory which has been so gloriously won by Your Gallant Forces in conjunction with their brave Allies.'[12] And then, the following month, business as usual, and somewhat to greater effect than the efforts of former councils in many fields of municipal activity, not least for borough extension and for education. This latter cause of 1919 was highlighted recently for the county as a whole when the former Clerk of the County Council, E.R. Davies, compiled a history of the County Council since its formation. In 1919 he saw the chief single duty of the County as being to implement the Education Act of 1918, which raised the school leaving age to 15 and provided for special schooling for handicapped children.[14] Heavy as the price paid by the nation for victory in 1918, it is important to notice this special impetus in the area of education – paralleled in 1946 by a rather similar determination to implement the even more radical Butler Act of 1944.

References

1 WEE, 9 Oct. 1915.
2 BRO.
3 ibid.
4 The memorial to those Windsor people killed in the Second World War at Windsor Parish Church names some 116 members of the armed forces and 8 civilians.
5 BRO.
6 H. Nicolson, *King George V*, (1967 ed.), 405.
7 ibid.
8 BRO.
9 See the original MS speech in BRO.
10 Established on 9 May 1917, BRO.
11 WEE, 16 Nov. 1918.
12 BRO.

(iv) Between the Wars

This was national policy. For Windsor the more specific and local cause tackled in the inter-war years between 1919 and 1939 was the continued, though far from complete, eradication of the Victorian slums. The Sanitary Inspector and Stoneham between them convinced the Council that there was overcrowding in Oxford Road, unhealthy conditions in Sun Passage, and an 'appalling condition of housing in River Street.' In 1923 the Council declared the River Street warren of houses unhealthy and ordered an improvement scheme.[1] This was rapidly approved by the government. But if houses were demolished by Council order, houses would have to be built by the Council for those evicted. Such houses had begun to be constructed at Clewer Avenue in 1920 and in 1924 an attempt in new construction methods was made. Plans were formulated then abandoned for 6 concrete houses at Dedworth on the dust destructor site, and this had evolved into a plan for 58 cottages by 1925, 50 to re-house the River Street inhabitants.[2] In 1926 a car park and a public lavatory replaced the River Street slums. By this time the idea of council houses was gathering momentum. Negotiations

Lt. Col. Sir Arthur Churcher, Mayor 1935 and 1936, and other civic dignitaries led by Charles Mulford and Macebearer, the Town Clerk (small wig) J.W. Hambidge, and the Recorder (full wig) Hugh Murray Sturges, K.C.

began in 1926 to purchase part of Vale Farm in Dedworth,[3] and a year later the Minister of Health approved the building of 144 houses there.[4] In 1930 closing orders were made for houses in Sydney Place, Acre Passage, South Place and Clarence Clump.[5] In 1934 negotiations began to acquire part of Church Farm, Dedworth, in order to erect 66 houses for 203 displaced persons.[6] And so the process continued: Sun Passage, Charles Street, even parts of St Leonard's Road were demolished. Independent builders such as Messrs. Varney and Messrs. Foreman built houses, still highly identifiable in style on former private estates. Windsor grew its own suburbs between the wars stretching towards the Maidenhead boundary on the west and to the beginning of Crown lands adjacent to the Long Walk on the south. The council building projects owed much to local initiative, but depended on the impetus provided and the power granted by the two Housing Acts of 1920 and 1930, which included authority to raise loans.

Inter-war urban growth and improvement were not solely on the perimeter. The inner town did not escape development. Sheet Street was widened, the bottle-neck at the top of Peascod Street eliminated (by the destruction of rather fine timber-framed shops on the south); the river front was further improved and the 'Goswells Meadow', already a National Trust property, was transferred to the management of the Corporation, but there was a price and not all Windsor people were happy as rather shoddy new premises appeared, for instance, in Peascod Street following street widening. 'Windsor Ratepayers' in May 1935, petitioned the Council to allow 'quaint' old buildings in Peascod Street and elsewhere to remain, and where re-building was necessary to maintain harmonious likeness of style with the old buildings.[7] This advice the Council merely 'noted'. And it is the sad fact that no building between 1919 and 1939 equalled the standard set by the Edwardian public and private buildings. The slums went; and very un-distinguished shops, chain stores and council houses came. Considerations of architectural style did not become prominent until the 1950s.

Anyhow, the Council was in business in fact extremely adroit. Carter was still presiding over much of its work as Mayor from 1923 to 1927, and on his retirement in 1932 his successor, Alderman Rawkins, took the opportunity of making the Mayoral election a more public and solemn occasion. He therefore invited pupils from the local schools to the Guildhall for the ceremony on the 9th November.[8] Rawkins drew attention to a 14 year old boy there with them, 'Master Smith', who had represented England in an International Oratorical competition in the U.S.A. Rawkins told Smith that one day inspired by the mayor-making, he himself might achieve the mayoralty. Little did Alderman Rawkins know! Charles Smith, from a triumphal career at the County Boys School under Gammon and his notable successor, Herbert Fairhurst, gained a scholarship to Wadham, Oxford at the early age of 16; became Member of Parliament for Colchester and ultimately a life peer as Lord Delacourt-Smith, and a senior member of the Labour Government. In the present writer's opinion, he was the most effective Front-Bench speaker in the House of Lords of the Labour Party in the post-war period until his sadly early death at the age of 55, by which time he was ready for one of the highest ministerial posts. Charles Smith (in the epoch of 'initials only', known as C.G.P.S.) was the town's outstanding home-bred politician in this or any other century, and a witness to the educational standards of the Boys' School in the Gammon-Fairhurst epoch.

But although born locally (the son of the manager of Neville Reid's brewery at Riverside) and throughout his life owning a house in Osborne Road, Charles Smith did not in fact join the Council – he became a governor of the Girls' School, and his wife, a Justice of the Peace. The Council was to contain, however, several of the able schoolmasters who had taught him, and throughout the mid-twentieth century the Council tackled with competence the business of turning a part-time, not very well-run, administration into an effective piece of local government. The starting point was the building and inspection of property.

There was in fact so much building to erect or to inspect that in 1925 the Borough 'Surveyor', E.A. Strickland, was re-entitled the Borough 'Engineer'. Then in 1929 the Borough appointed a specialist Town Clerk. Until then the Town Clerks had been private solicitors, managing the town's affairs from their private offices. Mr J.W. Hambidge on 16th January, 1929, became full-time Town Clerk; next month he was given a 'competent shorthand typist' and an office provided at 14 Park Street.[9] The Borough Accountant had done his work hitherto in the Police Station; he also moved to Park Street. This was a beginning, if an incredibly belated one, and after the Second World War a more substantial effort was subsequently made to provide a centralised administrative office which would also include the Borough Engineer.

But shadows were falling. In spite of received historical wisdom that no preparations of any substance were made for possible attack in the aftermath of Hitler's coming to power, it is interesting to note that on 9th October, 1935, Windsor Council appointed a sub-Committee to plan air raid precautions,[10] and in 1936 the town was certainly being prepared for air-raids. A Warden was appointed in February, 1937,[11] and of course by 1938 trenches were being dug and cellars prepared. At first, it was thought Windsor would be very much at risk in a war. Mr Hambidge as Town Clerk advised in January 1939 that with its Castle, its garrison, and its proximity to London, Windsor would suffer and certainly should not receive refugees.[12] The government disagreed. Windsor was merely a 'neutral' area and was generally considered a 'refuge'. Events proved that neither side in the argument was completely right.

Life in the inter-war period was not all housing and air-raid precautions. It was, in fact, one of the relatively halcyon periods in Windsor's history. The massive unemployment of the 1930s was little felt and the town, slightly off the main routes and protected by the 19th century half-circle of Crown Lands, led a quiet life, slightly London-oriented, and became an agreeable commuter land. The musical and artistic life already described flourished; the Royal Albert Institute continued to offer club rooms, a library and a complex lecture programme; sporting clubs were almost at their apogee. And, significantly, in 1933 a 'Windsor Free Library' was opened after generations of hostility to such a thing, dating back to the refusal of a Carnegie Library in 1903. The Mayor, in opening it, commented that Windsor's educational system 'had been re-organised and brought up to date in recent years' and this development would be crowned by the establishment of a free library.[13] Between 2 and 3 thousand volumes became the stock of part of the old 'British School' in Victoria Street. The

Library, now moved to St Leonard's Road is certainly a vital amenity, with both a children's department and a well-stocked reference section (but still needs expansion).

Two great public occasions distinguished the inter-war years; the Pageant of Runnymede in 1934, mainly commemorating the agreement of Magna Carta in 1215[14] and the Royal Progress through Windsor of King George V and Queen Mary in 1935 to celebrate 25 years' reign. A River Carnival and the flood-lighting of the Castle for the latter emphasized Windsor's historic life as a river port and as a royal home.[15] With ARP (that is, Air Raids Precautions) coming the next year, it also virtually constituted a climax and conclusion to two decades of vigorous and successful municipal development.

References

1 BRO.
2 BRO.
3 BRO.
4 ibid.
5 BRO.
6 BRO.
7 BRO.
8 WEE, 11 Nov. 1932, the mayor-making following Sir William Carter's death on 14 Oct.
9 BRO.
10 BRO.
11 BRO.
12 BRO.
13 BRO.
14 ibid., WEE, 1934.
15 ibid.

(v) The Second World War

War was declared on 3 September, 1939. The first outward sign in Windsor was the setting up of a Food Control Committee of 5 representatives of the trade and 10 Councillors, with the task of registering and licensing retail dealers, of controlling the transfer of customers, and of inspecting records. A Food Office was opened; ration cards were issued to residents.[1] Soon Windsor began to function as a 'refuge'. Several thousand children had arrived by June, 1940; they came to the railway station, were there 'labelled', and those clear of illness proceeded to Bachelor's Acre for distribution.[2] By January, 1941 billets had been found for up to 5000, though then more than a hundred evacuees were still camping out in a hall.[3] A 'community restaurant', the British Restaurant, was opened at 127 Peascod St, with a main course for 8d. or 10d. – there were 239 dinners the first day and the Restaurant continued until May, 1945 as a useful social service.[4]

But the idea of Windsor as a safe area was almost as erroneous as the Town Clerk had prophesied. In September 1940 bombing led to the destruction in Alma Road, Goswell Road and Bridgewater Terrace. In December of that year bombs fell on houses in Goswell Rd., and hundreds of bombs fell, if harmlessly, in the area of the Great Park.[5] High explosive bombs continued to fall erratically on Windsor from 1941 to 1943, 20 bombs for instance falling on the Albert Street – Vansittart Road area in February, 1941 and some on Kings Road – Helena Road in January, 1943.[6] Then in 1944 flying bombs led to 202 alerts – one flew into the dust destructor chimney, others landed daily at what seemed to be the end of their run, along a line from Wraysbury to the Bells of Ouseley and Beaumont College, with some deaths, many casualties and damage of varying degrees of seriousness, to a thousand or more houses in Windsor and its immediate district.[7]

The defence of Windsor was partly in the hands of Local Defence Volunteers (subsequently the 'Home Guard') partly under an Air-Raids Precaution Committee with a Report Centre in Victoria Street under the old Burges' Brewery, a Chief Warden's Office in Trinity Place, and some 200 voluntary wardens.[8] The fire service not only dealt with the local incidents. In 1941, for instance, groups of Windsor firemen went to Bristol, Liverpool and Manchester, sometimes fighting fires for 10 hours or more.[9]

Windsor is not, however, likely to figure very prominently in the history of the Second World War with a single exception only: that one of its former schoolboys contributed outstanding pieces of design for the Royal Air Force. Sydney Camm, one of five sons of an Alma Road family had been to school at the Royal Free School and while there he made model aircraft. By the age of 18 Camm had built a full-size glider, which was exhibited at the Royal Agricultural Show in the Home Park (in 1911). He became a woodworker, and then a draughtsman in the aircraft industry, joining the Hawker Aircraft Company in 1924. His first great triumph was to produce the Hawker Hurricane in 1936 – and by 1939 more than a thousand a year were being made. One of the leading fighter aircraft of World War II, it gained fame most notably in the desperately fought encounter of the Battle of Britain. The Hurricane was followed by the Hunter, and at his death, in 1966, Sir Sydney (as he became) was working on vertical take-off aircraft. *The Times* called him 'one of the most consistently successful designers the aircraft industry has ever had' who triumphed 'without making a false step'.[10] Eccentric, aggressive, a loner, he was something like a genius – and probably ranks with Edmund Fellowes, in a rather different creative field, sharing with him similar personality characteristics, as one of Windsor's two great men of the twentieth century. David Mondey has pointed out that Camm's creation of the Hurricane was typified for many years after peace had come by the fact that 'a lone Hurricane had the honour of leading the R.A.F. fly-past over London' to commemorate the Battle of Britain.[11]

But it was clear that if Windsor after 1939 was not a refuge, it never became as such an enemy target. The Royal Family, as we have seen, came to Windsor to find rest from constant attacks on London; the work of the town continued, and in addition to direct war service its inhabitants concentrated on raising money for war supplies. A War Weapons Week in June 1941 set a target of £125,000; in the same month nearly three-quarters of a million pounds were invested in War Bonds, and special weeks were organised; A Russian week in October, 1941 when all members of the Council sent a message to M. Maisky by admiring 'the magnificent resistance of the Soviet people to the Fascist invader', signed by most adults in the town.[12] A Warship Week in February, 1942, raised £349,000;[13] a Book Recovery and Salvage Drive (slightly disastrous perhaps in some ways) took place in February, 1943;[14] a Wings for Victory Week in May, 1943;[15] a Salute the Soldier Week in February, 1944[16] and so on. The May 1943 effort had long-term results. In addition to a circus, concerts, a rabbit show and a Grand Parade there was a 'Horse Show' (on May 26th). This last event was a splendid success. The Duke of Kent and Princess Alexandra attended and the feeling was that it 'equalled any peace time display'.[17] With us still today, the 'Royal Windsor Horse Show' in the Home Park with five-day events now has become the biggest and best of the national horse-shows, since 1970 being followed by the Windsor International Driving Grand Prix.

Other efforts to make up for long hours of work, rationing and frequent air raid alerts included the idea of 'Holidays at Home' – again centering on the Home Park, with massive community efforts to produce moderately entertaining fancy dress shows, tennis tournaments, horticultural shows, brass band concerts.[18] But these proved a relative failure. Councillor Surplice acidly remarked that you do not get a holiday by staying at home.[19] But as the war seemed to be running in the allies' favour, more forward planning for victory developed than had been seen in the First World War. In 1943 a Home Nursery was organised[20] and in February 1944 a centre was opened in Queens Road – a Social Services Group, conscious of Windsor's shortage of housing, produced a statement on 'The Evils of Overcrowding' in that year.[21] in the same year the result of County Boys School staff room thought, 'Planning for the future of Windsor' was issued.[22] This helped a movement towards social reform in the Council, which in October 1944 described a 'Windsor in 1970' which would have new estates and, in the words of Mrs Bourne-May, 'Every child within walking distance of a garden big enough for a playground'.[23] A Social Centre and a new Library were proposed and in 1945 Sir Owen Morshead, as we shall see, asked for a 'Civic Society' to foster the artistic and

The late Sir Owen Morshead, Librarian Emeritus to Her Majesty the Queen.

environmental life of Windsor and Eton. Finally, the senior school of the Imperial Service College having left Windsor in 1942, its buildings although requisitioned and used by the Ministry of Defence were ear-marked both for housing development and for a much needed municipal centre.[24]

Catastrophic as had been the sufferings of all nations during the war, there had been engendered some belief in communal effort as well as in central control that was going to have an effect on national politics when the post-war election was held, and certainly had encouraged locally an impulse towards greater civic enterprise.

References

1 WEE, 8 Sept. 1939.
2 ibid., 14 June 1940.
3 ibid., 10 Jan. 1941.
4 ibid., 29 June 1941; 25 May 1945.
5 ibid., 27 Dec. 1940.
6 See the record of Windsor war damage, no. 2 (1941 – 5), BRO.
7 cf. entries in BRO and WEE, June – August 1941.
8 WEE, 19 June 1940; 10 Jan. 1941.
9 ibid., 10 Jan. 1941.
10 The Times, obituary, 1966; see also Camm papers, BRO. Camm was in fact not the only Windsorian to pioneer in aircraft design – Patrick Young Alexander was working (though less successfully) on balloons, gliders and other forms of aviation from the pre-1914 years, and acquired considerable fame. We await his biography by Gordon Cullingham; see Alexander papers, BRO.
11 D. Mondey.
12 WEE, 6 June 1941; 13 June 1941; 3, 17 Oct. 1941.
13 ibid., 6 Feb. 1942.
14 ibid., 26 Feb. 1943.
15 ibid., 22, 29 May 1943.
16 ibid., 18 May 1944.
17 ibid., 29 May 1944.
18 ibid., Aug. 1942 issues; July 1943 issue.
19 ibid., 24 Sept. 1943.
20 ibid., 12 Nov. 1943.
21 ibid., 12 Nov. 1943; 17 March 1944.
22 ibid., 19 May 1944.
23 ibid., 20, 27 Oct. 1944.
24 ibid., 1 March 1946.

(vi) Re-organisation

In August 1945, Japan surrendered. Windsor's church bells rang in celebration. A torch light procession, bonfires, riverside lights, fireworks, helped to produce a fairly general euphoria. And the sense of a new order, or at any rate, new possibilities, came with the election nationally of a Labour majority for the first time in the House of Commons and in Windsor of a Labour majority of two on the Town Council, which then proceeded to choose 5 Labour Aldermen.[1] Alderman Fred Fuzzens became Windsor's first Labour Mayor in November 1946.[2] In 1945 a Labour Party pamphlet 'Your Windsor' had included a pictorial version of 'Windsor of the Future' with a new bus and shopping centre, a relief road and 'Windsor Gardens' – some of which was in fact achieved. Locally, the Labour party majority was short-lived. In November 1946 it lost its majority,[3] but several of the new Labour Councillors remained prominent in Windsor affairs to the last days of the Borough in 1974, when Alderman John Procter, another Labour Mayor, fought strongly to prevent an amalgamation of Windsor and Maidenhead in the interest of a sense of an historic tradition of civic independence.

The Conservative majority was equal in its capacity to provide distinguished leadership. In particular, Alderman Richard Tozer, Mayor from 1949 to 1952, 'raised the Mayorality to a height which his successors will find difficult to maintain' as the local paper remarked. A man of the right, he came to resent constant party bickering (particularly noticeable in the 1950s) and his individual impartiality and rugged independence were outstanding – as was his energy, with some 3,000 official engagements in the Festival of Britain Year of 1951.[4]

Official activity after 1946 was paralleled by a more general growth in popular civic consciousness. This was undoubtedly led by Sir Owen Morshead, Royal Librarian from 1926 to 1958. On 19 December 1945 Morshead chaired a discussion at the Theatre in order to form a Civic Society, and on the following 18 January 1946 the Society was constituted at a meeting in the Guildhall with Morshead as President, R. Weatherall, an Eton master, as Chairman, and Raymond South, from the Boys' Grammar School as Vice-Chairman. The Society has flourished vigorously ever since, providing lectures and visits for its members, and through a sub-committee formed in 1964 keeping an ever-vigilant eye on planning developments. Thus in 1973 the Society reported that this sub-committee had by then held one hundred meetings, and had sponsored the registration of Bachelors' Acre as a Town Green, ie a public place not to be used (as the Corporation had in fact been using it) as a car park. The Society was successful, and by 1983 the Acre had become once more an agreeable central recreation area. Meanwhile, a Landscape sub-committee was

Aerial view westwards of the Thames flooding of March 1947.

struggling with problems of tree conservation and another group had arranged concerts which included a lecture-recital by Gerald Moore, and a performance by Paul Tortellier in St George's. The Windsor and Eton Society mobilises public opinion and brings together Eton, the Chapel and the Borough in the tradition formed a century earlier by the Victorian music societies, but with far wider social and civic aims. One of its most distinguished, active and irrepressible members, Miss Doris Mellor, MBE, set up the 1963 sub-committee and personally monitored every planning development for about twenty years. She died in 1980 and is commemorated by 'Mellor House' in Peascod Street, and by the survival of the Acre as an open space. The work of the Society is now admirably complemented by the Windsor Community Arts Centre which was founded in 1975 and moved to the old Police Station in 1981. A two month programme in 1983 revealed activities ranging from Contemporary Dance and a Rock Night to film and dramatic productions. This is one of Windsor's achievements of the decade.

Unfortunately, one of the earliest post-war voluntary achievements proved relatively short-lived. A 'Bygone Windsor' arranged by the Windsor and Eton Society[5] in 1949 had led to the establishment of a permanent local history museum in the Guildhall which was opened on 15 May 1951 (as part of the general restoration of the Guildhall area by a Council Committee) by Princess Elizabeth.[6] Maitland Underhill, F.S.A., the brilliant Hon. Secretary of the Berkshire Archaeological Society, became its first Honorary Curator, and for a generation the Guildhall with its attractively designed exhibition was open to the public during the summer months. It was here, for instance, that the startling discoveries from Kingsbury, could be displayed and interpreted. Annually schools sent parties of children in the autumn to learn something of the town's heritage. After local government re-organisation in 1974, however, the Exhibition seemed to have less relevance to the wider district under whose management it fell; recession, anyhow, meant fewer visitors and an increased charge on the rates. The Exhibition was therefore closed in 1982, appropriate items being offered to the Queen Victoria exhibition mounted by Madame Tussauds at the Western Region Station. This closure followed another equally inevitable retreat from the expansionist policies of the late 1940s. From 1947 the borough had made all its historical records available to the public in the Guildhall, under the supervision of another honorary Curator (or, rather archivist). When the Kipling Building was acquired, more recent records – a vast bulk – were also stored there. Local history groups, genealogists and well-known historians came regularly to use the Windsor documents. Then, when the Kipling Building was demolished in 1981 as no alternative accommodation within the borough could be afforded the County Record Office (which by then had acquired first-rate accommodation in the new building at Shire Hall, Shinfield Park, Reading) agreed to take the Windsor records. Their archivist followed them on appointment as honorary Consultant to the County, and the Windsor Charters, deeds and the many personal deposits now enjoy air-conditioning and expert management in the custody of the County Archivist. Much of this book has been based on these extensive borough records (as the many BRO references indicate).

To produce a balanced estimate of local government attitudes, however, it is necessary to survey the wider and impressive activity of councillors (both pre-1974 and since) on the social and planning front. By 1946 it had become clear to all political parties, as we have seen, that Windsor needed 'development'. Firstly, it was essential once more and, this time, finally, to eliminate the Victorian slums. A slum clearance plan of 1952[8] led to more demolition orders, mainly in Clewer New Town, but also nearer the centre as in Sun Passage, of houses unfit for human habitation. Secondly, more housing estates were needed for both the displaced and the overcrowded; some came from private builders, others from council development – there was still in 1954 a housing list of 500 applicants.[9] But by and large, Harold Macmillan's reputed if apocryphal 'you have never had it so good' was partly echoed in Windsor – in 1953 it was claimed that Windsor was a

A changing of the Guard in July 1982.

town practically without unemployment. Men found employment at Slough and in London as well as locally; women began to staff hotels and shops in large numbers.

But environmental officers and councillors of 1946 – 50 were dissatisfied. This was papering over the cracks, making good the deficiencies of the past. Robert Hening and Anthony Chitty produced the first Development Plan for Dedworth-Clewer in 1946,[10] emphasising the need for some industrial base for Windsor life. A radical, indeed revolutionary resident had once advocated the clearance of the cobbled streets and the destruction of the Guildhall itself to provide gardens between the Castle and the Parish Church. A rather more authoritative Windsor Development Plan of July, 1950 called for flood banks, a relief road, a central bus station on the Acre, and the formation of a Windsor industrial area – Windsor should not simply be a tourist attraction and a service provider.[11] In 1953 pleasure grounds with a zoo on the river bank were suggested,[12] and in 1954 redevelopment of the 'inner-city' area of Victoria Street and Peascod

Street.[13] Replanning of the centre of the town featured in reports of 1966[14]

The outcome of the plans of the 1950s in the following 20 years has been considerable, if not overwhelming. Intolerable traffic congestion, together with the structural weakness of the Windsor – Eton bridge,[15] led to a circulation system with a new bridge to the west of the town which is linked to the Bath Road, the M4, and so to Heathrow Airport. Central Windsor itself therefore, could be by-passed and a pedestrian way established near the old bridge. Light industry began to appear in western areas of the borough; the riverside walks were improved moderately, although hardly up to the standard of the nearby Alexandra Gardens. Above all, large chunks of Victorian Windsor were rebuilt. The remaining sub-standard Goswell streets provided a site for 'Ward Royal', a complex of flats which gained (surprisingly) a national prize.[16] A major shopping centre costing £10 million (King Edward Court) in 1979 formed between Ward Royal and Peascod Street under a partnership agreement with the Prudential Association has proved notably popular and gained a top environment award;[17] two other small courts of new shopping areas were built off Thames Street; and at many points from Sheet Street to Farm Yard large blocks of office accommodation were provided in the 1970s and 1980s for London and International business companies. The 19th century British School, Congregational Church, Post Office, Royal Albert Institute, and the riverside Brewery have yielded to highly contemporary purple-red brick blocks of buildings. Occasionally, as in Thames Street and Victoria Street, old facades have been skilfully disembowelled to enable modern accommodation to establish itself behind. Never has Windsor experienced so much non-domestic building in its nine centuries of life as between 1950 and 1980.

There has been much gain. The slums have at last gone. No 'inner-city blight' has resulted. The M4 and Heathrow have brought Windsor into the main current of international business life (one only needs to look at the brass name-plates, for instance, along Park Street). Windsor thus now is not just a Castle accretion, or a London outer suburb. It has some light industry, a great deal of international finance and national headquarters for various societies. And of course, it still needs its hotels and shops for nearly 3 million annual tourists from all over the world.

The loss of the last decades is less clear. Of course, the business people leave their offices and usually the town itself after 5.30 or 6 p.m. Few are Windsor residents or participants in Windsor life; this is an 'inner-city blight' of a sort, and the *Express* in 1983 reported a 'major clampdown' on office development as almost 100,000 square feet of existing accommodation was unused.[18] The new office buildings themselves have avoided the 'unfriendly and crude' mannerisms Lutyens thought to be features of so much 20th century buildings, and now have made cautious efforts at 'local vernacular', suggesting a return to Norden's half-timbered houses, not high-rise, often irregular in facade, quirkish and domestic in character and largely un-ornamented (our century has been starved of ornament). The general feel is that of a series of rather whimsical farm-houses. Well-built, no challenge to the Castle, but as unoriginal for the most part as had been the Victorian neo-gothic. Admittedly, architecture is a controversial matter, but, to some, Windsor streets now seem rather motley. In the centre is an amalgam of chain stores of pre-1939, and of modish neo-vernacular cottagy offices of post-1946, dotted here and there with the occasional survivor of the mediaeval or the Regency past. Not coherent, nor particularly beautiful, but representing a continuing adaptation to what seem to be current needs, generation by generation, and never challenging the splendour of the Chapel and Castle.

Windsor as we have seen has its civic society, the Windsor and Eton Society; it retains its Horse Show; it now has a world famous Safari Park and a splendid Windsor Festival of the arts in September; the long and brilliant Theatre Royal tradition continues. The stimulating Community Arts Centre since 1980 is doing valuable work in the Edwardian Police Station, and the Imperial Service College eventually (in 1950) became an administrative centre for the Borough. Dramatic changes have resulted from the Local Government Act of 1972 and the abolition in 1974 of the historic Royal Borough of New Windsor. By modern standards the Borough population of 28,000 had been too small to support the necessary services and staff – uneconomic. And it was too urban; there was a real call for greater integration of rural and town life. But should Windsor remain the centre, with a cluster of villages to the west and south drawn into its boundaries, or should Windsor join with Maidenhead (population 49,000) and take in appropriate rural areas? The latter plan triumphed; but the writer recalls, on the last day of the old order, John Procter the last Mayor of New Windsor walking despondently up and down the corridors of Kipling Building as office furniture and papers were removed to Maidenhead Town Hall exclaiming 'Oh, why did it have to happen?' and the charismatic Sir 'Kit' Aston, to be first Mayor of the new Borough had said in December 1973 'Nobody wanted it. This was forced on us.'[19] So, inevitably, 1974 was a climactic year. A town of 30,000 suddenly became a district of 130,000 – the most drastic change since Windsor moved to the chalk hill in about 1100. The short passage of years since 1974 is not sufficient to enable any sort of balance sheet to be drawn up, especially as related alterations in the even older county boundaries are not yet widely accepted. But some administration which had been transferred in 1974 from Windsor to Maidenhead returned to Windsor when 'York House' was built in Sheet Street in 1980. Councillors meet still in Maidenhead Town

Peascod Street in the 1970s.

Hall but they gather in Windsor Town Hall for civic occasions and certainly for great Royal events. The new district council of 'Windsor and Maidenhead' was immediately made a Borough and, again, a Royal Borough.[20] Although hardly any simple 'borough consciousness' has developed, councillors from Wraysbury and Maidenhead have proved meticulous in seeking to attain Richard Tozer's assiduous encouragement to local societies and institutions. The town itself has suffered from recession. Pavements are cracked, weeds grow, hospital services are curtailed; other social services are scrutinised for economies. But Castle and Borough continue their busy life, increased by the new accessibility by road and air, by the establishment of the Safari Park on St Leonard's Hill, and not least by the frequent residence in the Castle of members of the Royal Family. When the present Queen, as Princess Elizabeth, opened the restored Windsor Guildhall in 1951, during the Festival of Britain, she told her audience that under restoration it had been found that 'the main supporting beam for the Guildhall was the trunk of a great oak tree which had been placed there 250 years ago![21] This, Princess Elizabeth felt, was a true symbol for our native institutions. It certainly is true for the Borough of Windsor itself. The historic development from the small Roman farming

Community at Old Windsor of nearly two thousand years ago to the castle, churches, factories and offices of today is long, but clear and continuous. The new Borough of Windsor and Maidenhead inherits the unofficial but valid title of 'historic'.

References

1 WEE, 7 Dec. 1945.
2 ibid., Oct. 1946.
3 ibid., 8 Nov. 1946.
4 ibid., 16 May 1952.
5 ibid., 18 Jan. 1946; and all the subsequent Annual Reports of the Society.
6 See the catalogue, 'Bygone Windsor' (1949); WEE, 18 May 1951.
7 Shelagh Bond prepared a *Handlist* of Windsor records in 1959 which was published by the borough, with an expanded second edition in 1973. Copies of this are available from BRO. As an offshoot of its archival activities, the borough has also published three volumes containing editions of the *Hall Books*, together with Mr Cullingham's volume on the Windsor Tapestries. It is encouraging that the new authority approved publication in 1983 – 4 of Miss Elizabeth Cuthbert's edition of the *Hall Book* for 1852 – 1874 (BRO).
8 WEE, 21 Nov. 1952.
9 On housing development see BRO.
10 Published by the borough (1946); see WEE, 20 Sept. 1946, 4 Oct. 1946.
11 WEE, 2 July 1950.
12 ibid., 2 Oct. 1953.
13 BRO.
14 BRO.
15 This historic line between Windsor and Eton was closed to traffic (though not to pedestrians) in April 1970.
16 Planning started in Jan. 1960; the buildings were completed in June 1967 at a total cost of £1,885,000. cf. WEE passim.
17 Plans for development started in March 1974; in 1983 the last constituent elements were being completed.
18 WEE, 2 Sept. 1983.
19 WEE.
20 The conferring of the title 'Royal' borough in 1922 was never officially recorded.
21 WEE, 18 May 1951.

Index

Acre Passage 154
Adelaide Square 92
Adelaide Terrace 92
Albany Road 142
Albert Road 11, 12, 102
Albert Memorial Chapel 19, 25, 82, 86
Alexandra Gardens 94, 148
Alexandra Road 122, 142
All Saints 109
Alma Road 108, 123, 158
Anson, Frederick 85
Atmospheric Railway 99, 102
Austin, E.H. 118

Bachelors Acre 115, 122, 157, 162
Baillie, Dean Albert 138
Barker, Mary 121
Barker, Mr Nutter 126
Barry Avenue 132
Barry, Francis 132
Bateman, Hon James 71
Beauclerk, Lord George 70
Beauclerk, Topham 71
Beaumont College 75
Bedborough, James Thomas 64, 92, 99
Bier Lane 94, 106, 108
Bier Street 35
Biggs, William 38
Blomfield, Sir Arthur 143
Blore, Edward 92
Bolton Avenue 130
Bolton Crescent 41, 130
Bolton Road 142
Bourne Avenue 142
Brakespear, Harold 134
Braye, Lord 144
Bridgewater Road 158
British School 123
Brunswick Terrace 92
The Bull 78
Bulstrode, Dr Timbrall 95, 98
Burford House 73
Burges' Brewery 149
Butchers Row 44

Camm, Sydney 158
Carlton, Geoffrey 26
Carter, Thomas Thellusson 111
Carter, Sir William 150
Castle Hill 35, 73, 102
Champagne, George 122
Chariott's Place 123
Charles Street 154
Chippys, Ralph 45
Chitty, Anthony 165
Church Lane 35, 122
Church Street 35, 55
Civic Society 162
Claremont Road 92
Clarence Clump 154
Clarence Crescent 41, 92, 94
Clarence Road 92, 123
Clayhill Farm 90
Cleaver, John 58
Clewer 16, 89
Clewer Brocas 71
Clewer Hill 35
Clewer Hill Road 89
Clewer House School 123, 125, 126
Clewer Park 102
Clewer Within 91
Colnbrook 51, 99
Congregational Chapel 116
Constitution House 116
Counsell, John 117
County Boys School 145, 146
County Girls School 147
Cromwell, Oliver 61
Curtis, Margaret 147

Dalton, Canon J.N. 85, 134
Darvill, Henry 97
Datchet 35
Datchet Lane 38, 51, 99

Datchet Mead 38, 57, 129
Davidson, Randall 84
Davie, Thomas 106
Davis, James 102
de Brocas, Sir Bernard 40
de Cygony, Engelard 20
Delacourt-Smith, Lord 155
Dering, Sir Edward 25
Duke of Roxborough 71
Dorset Road 92
Drapery Row 44
Dyson, Sir Charles Frederick 118, 149
Dyson, Cyril Douglas 149

Earl of Cardigan 71
Earl of Cholmondeley 70
Earl of Essex 59
Elvey, Sir George 84, 117
Emlyn, Henry 74
Eton College 41, 51, 99, 116, 128
Eton Excelsior Club 130
Everitt, M.C. 118

Fairfax, Sir Thomas 60
Fellowes, Dr Edmund 119, 139, 140
Fish Street 44
Fitch, Sir Thomas 64
Ford, Anne 57
Franklyn's Almshouses 54
Frogmore 36, 57, 99
Frogmore House 82
Fuzzens, Fred 161

Gallows Lane 38
Gammon, Sydney 119, 146
Gardner Cottages 132
Garter Festival 129
Garter Inn 57
Gibbons, Grinling 63, 109
Gibson, S.R. 146
Gloucester Square 92
Gooch, Daniel 102
Goodman, Sir Godfrey 58
Gordon, Robert 131
Gosset, Isaac 109
Goswells 38, 91, 95, 97
Goswells Meadow 154

Griffiths, Henry 75
Grove Road 92
Guildhall 44, 55, 64, 71, 78, 119, 145, 163
169
Gwynn, Nell 63

Hadleigh House 71
Hake, Edward 55
Hambidge, J.W. 156
Hartshorne's Inn 64
Harvey, Dr John 26
Hatch Lane 90, 111
Heald, Father Geoffrey 119
Hatton Hill 90
Hawtrey, Rev Stephen 117, 124
Hening, Robert 165
Hentnzer, Paul 56
High Standing Hill 90
High Street 33, 36, 44, 101
Hog Common 38
Hollis, Jesse 106
Holy Trinity Church 109

Imperial Service College 124

Kean, Edward 116
Keppel, Admiral Augustus 72
Kerridge, Mary 117
King Charles I 58
King Charles II 61, 63, 129
King Edward I 22
King Edward III 19, 23, 26, 47
King Edward IV 19, 29, 47
King Edward VII 136
King George I 69
King George II 69
King George III 72, 76
King George IV 73
King George V 137
King George VI 137
King Henry II 19
King Henry III 19, 29
King Henry VI 29, 47
King Henry VIII 51
King James I 57
King James II 61
King William I 14, 19

King William III 64
King Edward VII Hospital 145, 147
King, Bishop Oliver 25, 30
Kingsbury 12
Kings Road 92, 106
Kipling, Rudyard 125

Langley Park 71
Laud, William 58
le Ledeyatere, Henry 45
Longinotto, Canon 109
Lord Sidney 70
Lord Somerset 54
Luff, Councillor 145

Maisky, M 159
Marbeck, John 53, 54
Market House 44, 55
Market Street 35
Marshall, Edward 109
May, Hugh 62
Mechanics Institute 119
Mellor, Miss Doris 163
Melster, Thomas 53
Mere, William 40
Mill Common 64
Mill Lane 102
Monsell, Harriet 111
Moor Street 36, 54
Morshead, Sir Owen 140, 159
Municipal Buildings 149

National School 122

Ollard, S.L. 140
Osborne Road 90, 97
Outlivre, Mrs Susan Carol 116
Oxley, Richard 78

Page, Richard 57
Park Street 33, 36, 54, 102
Parratt, Sir Walter 84, 117
Peascod Street 36, 38, 40, 51, 71, 72, 77, 89, 92, 100, 165
Penn, William 106
Peyntour, John 45
Pilgrim Place 71, 77
Ponsonby, Sir Arthur 133
Porter, John 121
Pote, Joseph 78
Pound Street 44
Powney, Peniston Portlock 72
Price, Cornell 125
Pridie, George 77
Priest Street 121
Prince Albert 77, 81
Prince Consort Model Cottages 93, 131
Prince Charles 138
Prince Philip 138
Princess Charlotte 72
Princess Christian Nursing Home 83
Proctor, John 45, 162
Pucket's Close 54, 92

Queen Alexandra 136
Queen Anne 69
Queen Eleanor of Provence 22
Queen Elizabeth I 55
Queen Elizabeth II 138
Queen Katharine of Aragon 51
Queen Mary 136
Queen Victoria 73, 74, 81
Queens Road 125

Ramsbottom, John 131
Rawkins, Alderman 155
Rays Meadow 130
Reeve, Richard 71
Reeve, Sir Thomas 71
Richardson-Gardner, Robert 131
River Street 35, 94, 153
Riverside Station 38, 92
Roberts, Henry 93
Robins, Arthur 110
Royal Albert Institute 84, 119, 130, 146, 156
Royal Free School 121
Russell, Lord Wriothesley 85

St Agnes Church 41, 110
St Albans Street 35, 70
St Andrew's Church 33, 40, 104, 113

St George's Chapel 19, 23, 26, 29, 31, 47, 51, 53, 62, 74, 84, 86, 134
St George's House 139
St John Baptist Church 104
St Leonard's Road 41, 92, 125, 157
St Mark's School 123
St Peter's Hospital 41
St Saviour's Church 110
St Stephen's Church 109
St Stephen's College 111
St Stephen's High School 111
Savill, Sir Eric 138
Scheemakers, Peter 109
Schorn, John 29
Secker, John 93
Selwyn, George Augustus 109, 123
Sheet Street 38, 54, 71, 78, 90, 119, 154
The Ship 78
Shipley, Sir William 145, 149
Simons, William 53
Smith, Charles 155
South Place 94, 154
South, Raymond 162
Spital Hill 38, 90
Sponlee, John 26
Springfield Road 142
Stoneham, William George 94, 98, 151
Strickland, E.A. 156
Sturgis, Howard 144
Sun Passage 154
Surplice, Councillor 159
Swan Inn 35
Sydney Place 154

Temple Road 142
Tennant, Maraquita 111
Thames Street 33, 35, 40, 44, 51, 89, 99
Theatre Royal 116, 149
Thumwood's Barn 78
Tighe, Robert 99, 102
Tile Place Farm 11, 12
Tite, Sir William 92, 101
Topham, Richard 71
Tower, Canon Henry 111
Tozer, Richard 162
Trinity Guild 43
Trinity Place 92

Underhill, Maitland 164

Vansittart Road 158
Victor Road 142
Victoria Cottages 95
Victoria Street 92, 165
Victoria Street Dispensary 147

Wade, George 146
Ward Royal flats 167
Weatherall, R. 162
Wellesley, Gerald 84
Wellesley, Lord Charles 131
Wesley, John 108
West, A.W. 147
West, Sir Benjamin 74
White Hart Inn 82, 99
William IV Hotel 35
William Street 77, 106
Winkfield Road 90
Windsor Almshouses 92
Windsor and Eton Choral Society 117
Windsor and Eton Cricket Club 128
Windsor and Eton Football Club 129
Windsor and Eton Society 168
Windsor Community Arts Centre 163
Windsor Free Library 156
Windsor Rugby Club 129
Windsor Phoenix 129
Windsor Repertory Company 117
Woods, Dean Robin 138
Wren, Sir Christopher 61
Wyatt, James 74
Wyatville, Jeffry 74, 75

York House 168
York Place 92